WINE
WITH
FOOD

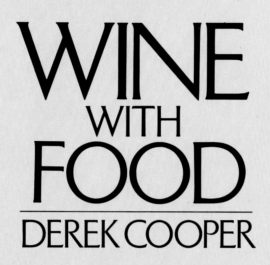

WINE
WITH
FOOD
DEREK COOPER

Crescent Books, New York

First English edition published by
Artus Books Ltd, 1980
First published in the United States of America
1980 by Crescent Books,
a division of Crown Publishers, Inc.,
by arrangement with Weidenfeld (Publishers)
Limited.
a b c d e f g h
CRESCENT 1980 EDITION

Printed in the United States of America

Contents

Introduction	7
The Joy of the Grape	13
The Making of Wine	21
A Guide to Taste	33
The Rituals	37
Reading the Bottle	49
Wine without Food	67
Wine with Food · 1	75
Wine with Food · 2	87
Wine in the Restaurant	103
Buying Wine	109
Wine and Health	113
Glossary	115
Vintage Chart	123
Further Reading	124
Acknowledgments	124
Index	125

Introduction

Why do we make such a drama about wine? We down beer without any fuss, choosing it more by the pub than the pint. We can make tea or coffee without embarrassment and drink it without a second thought. But wine. Oh, the doubts and uncertainties. Red or white? This one or that? Cut glasses or plain? Chilled or *chambré*? How worked up we get. But why?

The reasons are fairly obvious. Despite Britain's long commercial ties with the wine-producing countries of the world, the habitual drinking of table wine with food was until fairly recently restricted to a limited few. Like most people I was brought up in a house without a cellar. There was nothing under our stairs except a vacuum cleaner and a pile of old newspapers. My parents kept drink in the house but purely for medicinal purposes. A half-bottle of therapeutic brandy, a syphon of soda for dyspepsia, the remains of a bottle of green Chartreuse, some sweet sherry and that was it. At Christmas there was port and whisky and ginger wine and I do believe we drank something suitable with the turkey but I wouldn't swear to it.

And even now, after the wine explosion of the last few years, drinking wine in the home with a meal is exceptional, seldom the norm. In the wine-drinking Olympics, we don't even qualify. The Spaniards drink 70 litres a year each. The Argentinians drink 85, the Portuguese and Italians 91, the French 98. Yet in Britain, with all the wealth of wine at our disposal, we drink *less* than eight litres a year. In the United States the figure is lower still – less than six litres.

What we lack in thirst we certainly make up for in talking and writing. Every self-respecting newspaper and journal retains a wine writer and every year we publish nearly 100 books about wines and spirits. This is yet another. Of course I could make it a very short one by saying it doesn't matter what you

drink as long as you enjoy yourself in moderation. But that would not be quite honest.

It is a customary courtesy among those who take great care in choosing their food and drink to assure others that such care isn't really that important. Which is rather like saying that it doesn't matter if you turn up at a dinner dance in dungarees as long as you have a good time. In part, this is true. It doesn't *really* matter if you can eat kippers and bacon and eggs on the same plate and find it pleasurable. But if you're the sort of person who does care what you put in your stomach, as Dr Johnson did, this book will be a relaxing guide to the possibilities that exist when food and drink are combined in a way that is complementary to both. 'I look upon it', said Johnson, 'that he who does not mind his belly will hardly mind any-

thing else.' So let's admit that minding is important.

Just as some drinks complement others (wine doesn't mix very well with tonic water but doesn't come to grievous bodily harm when diluted with soda water; whisky is good with soda too, but horrid with tonic), there are certain foods that go uncommonly well with certain drinks. Fish and chips are perfect with a cup of tea; bread and cheese with draught bitter; curry and rice with lager. Coffee goes well with rolls and butter but imagine drinking coffee with pheasant or jellied eels!

Although we are still not what you might call a wine-drinking nation, even in the smallest towns we have a wider selection of wines to choose from than is to be found anywhere else in the world. Countries which grow grapes and make wine import it only in jealously limited

OPPOSITE *Most red wines reveal their full qualities when served at room temperature; most white wines, like the St Véran 1977 from Burgundy shown here in the ice bucket, are better chilled.*

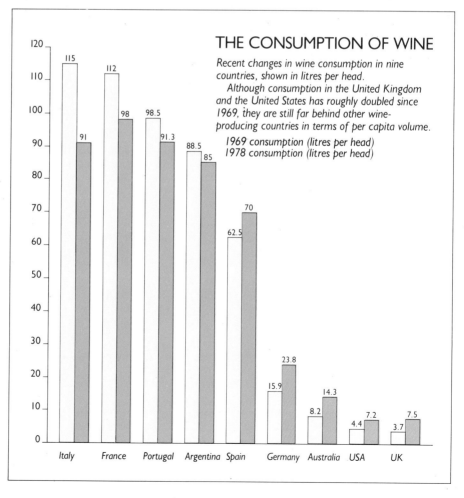

THE CONSUMPTION OF WINE

Recent changes in wine consumption in nine countries, shown in litres per head.
Although consumption in the United Kingdom and the United States has roughly doubled since 1969, they are still far behind other wine-producing countries in terms of per capita volume.

1969 consumption (litres per head)
1978 consumption (litres per head)

Italy 115 / 91
France 112 / 98
Portugal 98.5 / 91.3
Argentina 88.5 / 85
Spain 62.5 / 70
Germany 15.9 / 23.8
Australia 8.2 / 14.3
USA 4.4 / 7.2
UK 3.7 / 7.5

quantities. Go to Tuscany and you'll seldom be offered anything other than Chianti; go to Bordeaux and you'll drink claret. If you want anything other than the wine of the country you'll have to pay over the odds for it. But in Britain it's different.

For centuries Britain dominated world trade and her importers could afford to buy the best wines in the world. The cool damp cellars of London and Bristol proved ideal for keeping vintage wine and port until it reached its peak and we built up an unrivalled expertise in the selection and care of wine. We went further still, and created whole industries on the continent. In Cognac three of the best-known firms were founded by Britons: Thomas Hine came from Dorset, Jean Martell from Jersey and Richard Hennessy from Cork. In Oporto the names on the lodges of Vila Nova de Gaia reveal the English and Scottish origins of the port trade: Cockburn, Croft, Dow, Graham, Warre, Mackenzie, Taylor. In Jerez the sherry trade has been dominated for generations by firms with names like

Garvey, Williams & Humbert, Burdon, Croft, Harvey and Sandeman. In Bordeaux, a region which for three centuries was linked to the English crown, the British influence has been traditionally strong. It is because of these trade links with the wine producing countries of both the old and new world that today we import wine from 30 different countries in a bewildering variety of styles, blends and vintages. A small provincial wine merchant may stock as many as 300–400 different wines, and buying without expert knowledge at your elbow can be a daunting business. It seems as if it should be simple. Wine comes in only three colours – red, white and pink – and two conditions – still or sparkling. Yet red wine comes in shades ranging from brick-brown to purple. Pink or rosé can range from a pink the colour of boiled sweets to onion-skin brown. White includes every colour *except* white: straw, yellow, greenish, golden, amber. It is possible to draw many other distinctions: there are, for example, great wines, fine wines and everyday wines. The differences be-

ABOVE *Champagne has always been a luxury, chosen for celebrations. In the eighteenth century a bottle at the Pleasure Gardens in London's Vauxhall would have cost eight shillings compared with only two shillings for a bottle of port but, as today, it was the fashionable drink. Lord Chesterfield, the arbiter of Georgian taste, would cry: 'Give me Champaign (sic), and fill it to the brim, I'll toast in bumpers ev'ry lovely limb'. An engraving from the Champagne Museum at Épernay.*

OPPOSITE *The formal dinner party reached its zenith towards the end of the Victorian era, when those who could afford to sat down night after night to a succession of rich dishes and fine wines. At least four different wines and probably five or more courses would have been served with this meal. A late supper in the cardroom would have been provided for those feeling peckish around midnight. An illustration from the* Graphic *magazine by Arthur Hopkins, 1890.*

tween them, and the reasons for those differences, are quite an important part of this book.

It is because of these complexities that more and more wine is being marketed as simply and unpretentiously as possible. It is much easier these days to buy a bottle which proclaims in simple terms what it is and what it can be useful for: 'Dry red wine ideal with roasts and stews'. Shops, too, increasingly provide similar guidelines on their shelves. Yet international wine law still insists, in order to protect the consumer, that a great deal of information should be available on the label, and learning to read that label (see chapter 5) is an important step to a better understanding of wine.

The new branded wines are produced as consistently as possible from year to year and the one you bought last week will not be noticeably different from the one you bought the week before that. Useful wines for everyday drinking. This is the way the family buys the bulk of its wine in countries like France and Spain – ordinary red, white or pink wine

bought in large quantities for quaffing with the midday and evening meal. It's this range of medium-priced, unassuming wine that is the main growth area in both Britain and America, and we'll be looking at how they're made, what they taste like, how to recognize them and when to choose them.

Special occasions often call for something out of the ordinary – a wine not mass-produced but made with more than usual care and attention; the pick of the grapes, vinified carefully and allowed to mature and improve over a period of time in cask or bottle. It is these 'fine wines' that are the yardstick against which we measure the difference between the very best and the everyday. We'll look at Champagne and sparkling wines for celebrations, at fortified wines and some of the really great wines which are so unique and so limited in quantity that they command astronomic prices in the auction rooms of London and New York.

We'll also look at the conventions that surround the serving and drinking of wine, some of them logical, some of

them dotty. Since the eighteenth century wine-drinking has been the preserve mainly of the moneyed classes who until recently did little to discourage the emergence of rituals and tradition – surrounding your family with small snobberies with which only the initiated could cope was an invisible extension of the railings round one's park, designed to keep out the riff-raff.

The social distinctions concerning drink were elaborately constructed. Rich men drank vintage port; fallen women tippled port and lemon and navvies swilled beer. The rich had carriages and cellars full of fine claret; the poor went round to the 'Jug & Bottle' when they felt thirsty; the Mr Pooters of this world procured their Empire Burgundy a bottle at a time from the grocer round the corner.

Right until the mid-1950s a chain of wine merchants survived in the Surrey hills that was redolent, as estate agents say, of a more gracious and class-structured age. The shops themselves were more like consulting rooms than vulgar off-licences: oak-panelled

9

wainscots, thick carpets and solid Jacobean furniture. At a desk sat a sympathetic and deferential pin-striped gentleman with whom you discussed replacements for your cellar much as you might confer about an internal ailment in Harley Street. Money was not noticeably seen to change hands and deliveries were effected by van. It was a little bit of St James's in suburbia.

All that has changed but the small snobberies persist. Although enormous quantities of wine are being sold through supermarkets and chain stores there are still many people who have been made to feel inadequate when buying or choosing wine. Without a classical education at Oxbridge and a family background where the laying down of pipes of port on the arrival of the firstborn was mandatory, how can

you possibly talk about wine with confidence?

The same conventions applied to the 'marriage' of food and drink. In the Victorian and Edwardian eras, the leisured classes took great pains to wed food and wine together in as perfect a combination as possible. Sherry, Champagne, Madeira, claret, Burgundy and hock were paired with a succession of elaborate dishes. The rich stupefied themselves with conspicuous overconsumption and the new-rich created by the industrial revolution had to be taught by arbiters like Mrs Beeton how to take their place in a society which measured success by the degree of ostentation in the dining room. At grand banquets 30 or 40 dishes might be brought to the table and conventions arose about which wines were to be

proffered with which courses.

'It is generally admitted by real gourmets', wrote an authority in the middle of the nineteenth century, 'that red wines should precede the introduction of white wines.' Today the order is reversed and we drink white wines before red. In Victorian times it was customary to drink a very sweet white wine with a plate of oysters; today it would be both expensive and unthinkable. We reserve the sweet wines for the end of the meal. Taste has always been fickle; knowing what *not* to do was a full-time job.

'There has been of late years', wrote a Victorian cookery expert, 'a rage for dry wines of every description. This rage for dry wine, like most other fashions, was carried to an extreme, and was consequently followed by a reaction. The

Before dinner and after

ABOVE *The power of wine to loosen tongues has performed many a small social miracle over the centuries. A nineteenth-century engraving by George Cruikshank.*
OPPOSITE The Happy Gathering *by Jan Steen. Wine, women and song in seventeenth-century Holland. The owner of a tavern himself, Jan Steen is best known for his many humorous tavern scenes.*

rage for dry port has already ceased and probably before long there will be a slight reaction in the present rage for dry champagne.'

A hundred years later the taste of those who wish to appear sophisticated is once again for dry wines even though deep down they might actively prefer something sweeter. Nowadays, thanks to skilful marketing, it is possible for those with a zest for cream sherry to appear to be drinking dry sherry without having to forgo the pleasure of a sweet drink. Some years ago, one shipper managed to turn out a straw-coloured sherry – a blend of olorosos, amontillados and finos – that was as light in colour as a fino but had the comforting sweet taste of cream sherry. It was a clever concept, and now this 'fine old pale cream sherry' sells very well indeed.

The priorities of the palate are very much a result of social whims, and fashion is easily switched. As long as we remember the distinctions that ought to be drawn between what we like and what we think we ought to like then we'll preserve our sense of proportion and humour. Wine is there, like food, to be enjoyed; an occasion for relaxation. If we're going to worry about it then we'd be better off putting the corkscrew back in the drawer.

Unfortunately there are many books still in print concerned with the complexities of wine and food which might encourage you to throw the corkscrew in the dustbin and take to Valium. A lot of them, peppered with classical and literary allusions, give you the impression that you need a Ph.D. degree to really comprehend the joys of drinking.

Very few of us are going to be able to drink the really outstanding wines of the world; they are, like the Rolls Royce, relatively expensive and the demand far exceeds the supply. But even the drinking of an ordinary table wine can be enhanced by knowing what it is and why it tastes like it does. We shop around for our food with great care and so it should be with wine. With just a modicum of knowledge and a healthy curiosity the right wine can be found every time.

The Joy of the Grape

Why drink wine at all? There are several reasons and plenty of excuses. It is one of the most pleasant of God's gifts, it stimulates the appetite and enhances food. It promotes conversation and euphoria and can turn a mere meal into a memorable occasion. As the poet Horace put it nearly 2,000 years ago: 'Wine brings to light the hidden secrets of the soul, gives being to our hopes, bids the coward fight, drives dull care away and teaches new reasons for the accomplishment of our wishes.'

It has a magic about it and a mystery, but that shouldn't blind us to the down-to-earth fact that it is a very down-to-earth product: fermented grape juice.

There are about 50 different varieties of grapes commonly used in the making of wine and they vary from the tart to the deliciously honeyed. Each of them will make a wine with a particular taste. They are not unlike apples – put Bramleys in a pie without sugar and you'll get a very acid mouthful; stew Cox's Orange Pippins and the pie will be naturally sweet. Just as some fruits go better with cheese than others – we take an apple with Stilton, not an orange – so some wines, by the very nature of the grapey flavours within them and the way in which they have been made, are ideal partners for certain foods, poor for others. So let's look first at the raw material of wine, the grape.

Nobody knows from which particular part of the world the grape-bearing vine originally came, but man has been drinking wine with his food for at least 5,000 years and the antiquity of the custom goes back far beyond the days of ancient Greece to Egypt and the early civilizations of the East. The sacrificial wine which was offered as a tribute to pagan gods became the sacramental wine of the early Christian church. When we contemplate the wine in our glass we are looking at the oldest known agricultural product in the world which remains, despite the miracles of automated vinification and computer tech-

niques, a comparatively simple commodity.

Grapes grow successfully only in the sunnier parts of the world. As a fruit they need long hours of sunshine to bring them to ripeness, but excessive heat can be dangerous. They need the seasonal variations of the temperate zones to realize their full potential. In Europe the commercial grape-growing regions extend from the Midlands of England down to the coast of North Africa; in the United States vine–growing is possible in 28 states including the two most prolific, California and New York, which produce 96 per cent of all the wine made in North America. South of the equator there is another zone suitable for the cultivation of grapes. It lies between the 30th and 40th parallels and includes southern Australia, South Africa and the South American wine–making countries of Argentina, Chile and Uruguay. Within these well–defined areas there are a multitude of 'micro-climates' and soil variations which further determine the quality and quantity of grape production.

Every last bit of the grape has some commercial use. Even the skins, pips and stalks, the residue of wine-making, are returned to the ground as fertilizer or distilled into a fiery spirit known variously as *eau-de-vie de marc* in France, *grappa* in Italy, *bagaceira* in Portugal and *aguardiente de crujo* in Spain.

The pulp of the grape, composed almost entirely of water, also contains sugar and small quantities of acids, minerals and pectins, all of which determine the eventual quality of the wine. The stalk and the skin of the grape, black or white, contain tannin, an astringent substance which passes into the juice during vinification and gives character and long life to a wine. (See chapter 2 for a discussion of wine-making.) The more tannin a wine possesses the longer it will take to age, the more subtle its composition and the more durable its quality. Grape seeds also harbour tannin but great care is taken not to crush them when the juice is being extracted because they contain an

A cross-section of the grape.

vine leaf

skin

pulp

pips

stalk

oily resin which wouldn't do the wine any good. 'White' grapes range in skin colour from light yellow to deep green and 'black' grapes vary from red to a deep midnight hue.

From this single, simple fruit wine–makers the world over can produce wines of vastly different character and quality. The great wines – and here I'm thinking of those with names like Château d'Yquem, Château Lafite-Rothschild, Château Latour, Le Montrachet and Ockfener Bockstein Beerenauslese – are all made in small quantities and in the classic tradition. Some of them have been known to go on improving for decades. They command high prices and are seldom sold by ordinary wine merchants.

Fine wines, those which are made conscientiously and have an innate superiority about them, are more easily accessible. They usually, but not necessarily always, come from old established vineyards and over the years they have achieved respect and admiration for their honesty and integrity. In the United States fine wines are usually known as premium wines to distinguish them from mass-produced 'jug' wines made for party-drinking and thirst-quenching. Although the best fine wines are made in Europe an increasing amount of attention is being

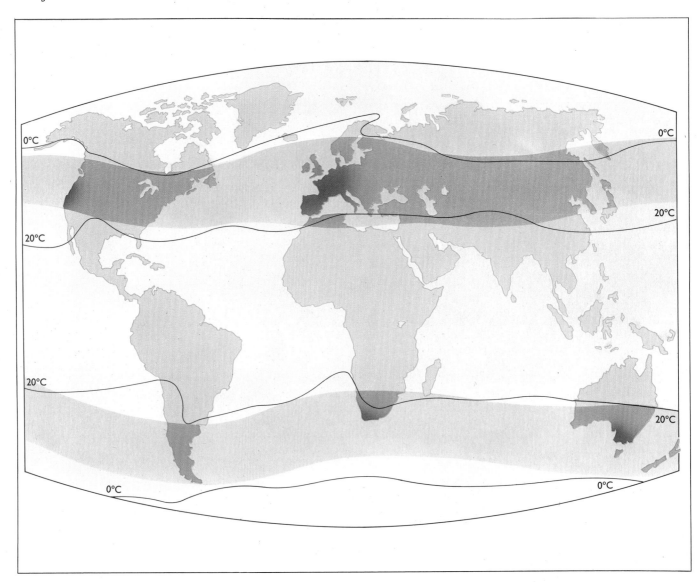

paid to quality elsewhere in the world and, even in Europe, areas not noted in the past for quality production are trying hard to raise their standards.

And then there are the everyday wines which can vary from the just drinkable to the very good indeed. These wines will lack the finesse and finish of fine wine; they will be less subtle, less complex in their flavour. They may well be more bland, more geared to a mass market. The French buy vast quantities of everyday wine under the name *vin ordinaire*. This is the category of wine that you will be offered when you go abroad – often brought to the table in an unlabelled bottle or carafe, filled from the patron's own barrel. It's the knock-backable, enjoyable wine that takes the place of water on the Mediterranean table. These commonplace wines will never win diplomas but they will in due course

lead many people on to a desire to taste something better.

Over the centuries some 8,000 different grape varieties have been evolved but the finest wines are produced from less than 50 vines, each of which has very individual characteristics. Frequently a variety of vines are cultivated in the same vineyard. This is particularly so in the more remote areas of Italy where farming is still almost biblical in its simplicity; one small patch may be providing corn for bread, olives for cooking oil and eating, and grapes for the table and for wine. In Greece, too, vines are as mixed, one with the other, as apple trees in a Devon orchard.

Some of the best-known wines in the world are a blend of grapes from different vines. Chianti Classico contains at least four different grapes: Sangiovese, Canaiolo, Trebbiano and Malvasia. That king of clarets, Château

The two bands indicate those regions of the world where the climate is suitable for growing vines. The darker areas within the bands are the major wine-producing areas. Isotherms, shown here in degrees Centigrade, are lines connecting places having the same average temperature.

Lafite-Rothschild, is made from Cabernet-Sauvignon, Cabernet Franc and Merlot. The finest Champagnes are blended from Pinot Noir, Pinot Meunier and Chardonnay. In the Rhône valley more than a dozen varieties of grape lend depth to the wines of Châteauneuf. Some give alcoholic strength, others aroma and bouquet, still others provide long life, colour and body. Although some of the finest wines are made from a single grape variety, blending to produce a balanced wine is a centuries-old art and the great wines of the world owe everything to the skill of their blending.

This seems an appropriate place to

*We talk about wine, the French tend to drink it.
Left, a French café, 1890; below, a street-scene at
St Malo, Brittany.*

make the distinction between wines which are named after the vineyard, château or domaine in which they are made; the geographical region where the vines are planted; some generic name hallowed by time; or (and this is increasingly popular) the variety of the grape from which the wine is made or the predominant grape in the blend.

In California, for instance, it is becoming more and more common to label the wine by its grape variety. These varietal wines, as they have come to be known, have taken the place of wines which were once somewhat hopefully described as Chianti, Chablis, Claret, Burgundy or Tokay. Thus on American wine lists you will see Beringer *Fumé Blanc*, Monterey Vineyards *Johannisberg Riesling*, Inglenook *Petite Syrah*, Château Montelena *Zinfandel*, or Joseph Phelps *Cabernet Sauvignon*.

In Europe a red Bordeaux wine could be generically described as 'claret', subdivided into Médoc, further identified by its commune (Pauillac, for example), and then ultimately identified by a vineyard, Château Fonbadet.

Similarly in Burgundy a wine could be Burgundy – from, say, the Mercurey district of the Côte Chalonnaise and from the vineyard known as Cornevent. If it were a lesser wine, it could of course simply be sold as *Bourgogne* or Burgundy.

Then there are wines like hock, Liebfraumilch and Bull's Blood which represent a particular type and style of wine.

However the wine is described, simply or elaborately, it is ultimately made of the product of a grape or blend of grapes, so let's look at two dozen of the most widely-grown grapes and see how they differ.

Aligoté This large white high-yielding grape is widely grown in Burgundy to produce Bourgogne-Aligoté, a pleasant medium-bodied dry crisp wine relatively low in alcohol which seldom improves after two years in the bottle. It is also found as far afield as Rumania and the Soviet Union. In Burgundy Aligoté vines are gradually being replaced when past their prime with Chardonnay.

Barbera The red grape grown mainly in northwest Italy in the Piedmont area; it also appears in California. Produces wines high in alcohol and light in colour.

Cabernet Main grape in the great blends of Bordeaux. There are two Cabernet grapes; the Cabernet Sauvignon, a small bluish-black, thick-skinned

Cabernet Franc

grape is grown widely in the Médoc area, while the Cabernet Franc predominates in Pomerol. The Cabernet grapes with their cedary, blackcurrant aroma are also found all over the world – the rest of Europe, California, South Africa, Australia and South America. They have a rich flavour and an intense bouquet, and demand long ageing to reveal their profound qualities. The juicy Cabernet Sauvignon grapes compose 90 per cent of the Château Mouton-Rothschild blend, a massive wine deep in colour, with a huge bouquet and a full flavour rich in fruit.

Chardonnay The grape from which all the finest white smoky wines of Burgundy are made: Meursault, Montrachet, Chablis, Pouilly Fuissé. Char-

Chardonnay

donnay flourishes on chalky soil and is the predominant vine planted in the calcareous soils of Champagne. A grape of delightful freshness, delicate fruit and a luscious potential which has been embodied in the great white wines of France, both still and sparkling. It has become California's most favoured varietal and is also planted extensively in Australia.

Chenin Blanc Another international vine best known in France for the wines of Vouvray, Côteaux du Layon and Savennières. It is so strongly associated with the Loire regions of Touraine and Anjou that it is sometimes known as the Pineau de la Loire or Blanc d'Anjou. The Chenin Blanc is one of the most versatile grapes that exists. Vouvray – the most distinguished white wine of Touraine and made entirely from the Chenin Blanc grape – can, depending on the vintage, emerge as a sweet, honeyed wine of remarkable complexity, a fruity bone-dry wine or virtu-

Chenin Blanc

ally anything in between. This grape also makes the excellent sparkling wines of the Loire whose production is centred round Saumur. It is found, too, in Australia, California and South Africa where in some areas a variation of the grape is called Steen.

Gamay The resident large black grape of Beaujolais; indeed many experts believe that it is such a fickle vine that it is only really happy on those granitic slopes. The wine is sold in Britain almost as a racing favourite – the November pilgrimage to Mâcon to bring back the first of the new vintage has become as silly as the August rush to

Gamay

dump the first grouse on a London restaurant table. Made for immediate drinking, young Beaujolais is a deep purple, fruity and quaffable wine which has become over-priced due to its fashionable over-attention. It also makes more serious wines such as Fleurie, Chiroubles, Juliénas, Chénas, and Brouilly. In California the Gamay grape grows extremely well.

Gewürztraminer A grape with a marked spicy aroma which offers an immediate and easily appreciated sensation of perfumed softness. The adjective *gewürz* means 'spicy' in German and it is perhaps an ideal wine for instant pleasure. Grown widely in Germany and Austria, sweet, fruity, fragrant and of low acidity, the Traminer reaches its greatest heights in the wine-producing areas of Alsace in northeastern France. In really warm years it can make a sweetish wine but it is usually fairly dry.

Gewürztraminer

Grenache Believed to be a native of Spain where it is grown in Rioja and Catalonia and is known as Garnacha or Alicantina, the Grenache has a fascinating repertoire. It is found in the wines of Châteauneuf-du-Pape, Bandol, Cassis, Gigondas, Fitou, Corbières and Minervois, and produces the famous pink wines of Tavel and Lirac and some of the sweet dessert wines of Roussillon and Languedoc in the south of France. It is also cultivated in Algeria, Morocco, Tunisia, Israel and Australia. It has a remarkable ability to thrive in even the hottest region. Introduced to the United States commercially in 1941 it makes a pink wine which has become a firm favourite in California, where nearly 20,000 acres of Grenache have been planted. The skins lack pigment and although its main role is as a blending wine it is a vigorous vine with a perfumed aroma.

Grenache

Malvasia A very sweet and juicy grape and a useful illustration of the way in which varietals alter from country to country. In Greece where it originated it was known as Monemvasia. In France it is called Malvoisie; in Spain Malvagia and it has given the English language the name for the sweet fortified amber-coloured dessert wines of Madeira which we call Malmsey. It was a butt of this rich wine that sadly engulfed the Duke of Clarence one damp day in 1478. In southern France the Malvoisie vine is the base for some sweet dessert wines (*vins doux naturels*).

Merlot One of the influential Bordeaux grapes, second only to the Cabernet. Château Petrus makes its wine with

Merlot

a 90 per cent Merlot concentration and in Bordeaux this bluish-black grape is prized for the softness and roundness which it contributes to Cabernet wines. Widely grown in Italy, especially in the north, and in Yugoslavia, Merlot thrives in Australia and South America.

Müller-Thurgau A light, flavourful, fruity grape low in acid with a hint of muscatel, developed in 1862 by Professor H. Müller from the Swiss canton of Thurgau. He crossed the Riesling vine with Sylvaner to produce a strain with such qualities that it provides a range of wines from the very dry to the very sweet. Although Müller's original intention was to combine the early-ripening, high-yielding Sylvaner with the healthy, highly-flavoured Riesling, he succeeded in producing so bountiful a vine that it now occupies 28 per cent of the vineyards of Germany. It is also widely planted in England.

Müller-Thurgau

17

Muscadet A grape introduced to the vine-growing region around Nantes in the western Loire by monks in the seventeenth century. Originally called the Melon de Bourgogne the vine has adapted itself particularly well to the Atlantic west of France and it has acquired a reputation as the ideal crisp and bone-dry white wine to accompany seafood. It can, when indifferently made, suffer from an excess of acid but as the growers will reveal to you it can also mature over the years into a wine reminiscent of a good white Burgundy. Unfortunately most Muscadet is consumed soon after its vintage.

Muscat A sweet grape, most commonly white, which occurs in several forms. It produces wines strong in perfume and honeyed fragrance such as Beaumes-de-Venise, Sétubal, Frontignan, Muscat d'Alsace, and Asti Spumante. An aroma mingled of roses and summer fruits makes the Muscat second only to Gewürztraminer in its distinctive assault upon the nose. The Muscat is also commercially used for grapes for the table and raisins for the kitchen.

Palomino A vine that thrives in hot climates, it has been cultivated for over 2,000 years in southwestern Spain, where it is the most widely grown grape in the sherry producing area of Jerez; it produces a pale, dry wine under the influence of the yeast known as *flor*.

Pinot Blanc Traditionally the Pinot Blanc was planted in Burgundy alongside the Chardonnay and in Chablis the local name for Chardonnay is Pinot Blanc. Though they are often thought to be related there is really no connection between the two grapes and it is not unlikely that the Pinot Blanc is a colour mutation of the Pinot Noir. In California Pinot Blanc has frequently been

Pinot Noir

Burgundy it reaches its peak to produce rich, smooth wines, deep red in colour. Some people are reminded of violets when they taste a well-made Burgundy, others of raspberries.

Riesling A versatile aristocrat which does for Germany what the Chardonnay does for France. The light yellow Rhine (or White) Riesling grape yields a fine, fruity, elegant and delicately fragrant wine in the Rhine, Mosel and Alsace, and its taste is easily appreciated. As Riesling, it appears under a variety of foreign guises: in Italy (Riesling Italico); Austria (Welschriesling); Hungary (Olasz Rizling); Rumania (Riesling de Italie); Bulgaria (Italiansky Rizling); Yugoslavia (Laski Rizling); Czechoslovakia (Rizling Vlassky) and the Soviet Union (Risling Italianski). It is also planted in nearly every other wine-growing country in the world where it makes wines which range

Muscat

Pinot Blanc

confused with Chenin Blanc so those whose eyes are becoming glazed should give up here! The Pinot Blanc has a distinct aroma and flavour and in Alsace it makes a crisp and acid wine ideally suited to the local food. It is also grown in Germany, Switzerland, northeast Italy and Chile.

Pinot Noir The traditional dark blue grape of Burgundy and Champagne; it has a remarkable aroma and is also grown in Germany under the name of Spätburgunder, in Austria (Blauburgunder) and in Hungary (Nagyburgundi). It produces the greatest wines of the Côte d'Or and the finest Champagne, and may well be the greatest black grape in the world. In

Palomino

Riesling

in colour from pale straw to rich gold. In America the Californians have crossed the German White Riesling with a Muscadelle de Bordelais to produce the Emerald Riesling. On some United States wine labels the legend 'Riesling' does not necessarily mean that the wine has been made from the White Riesling – it may be made from the Sylvaner grape, the Grey Riesling (the Chauché Gris vine of France) or the Missouri Riesling, a North American hybrid unconnected with the true Riesling. Whatever its background the word is pronounced *reezling*.

Sangiovese A fragrant grape full of flavour which forms the noblest part of the Chianti wines of Tuscany. The traditional blend is 70 per cent Sangiovese, 20 per cent black Canaiolo and a 10 per cent addition of Trebbiano and Malvasia but the proportions vary from grower to grower. Sangiovese is grown in many other parts of Italy including Sardinia, Emilio–Romagna, Latium and Campania but it seldom reaches the full beauty that it reveals in a Chianti Classico.

Sauvignon Blanc The leading white grape of Bordeaux, it also appears in the upper Loire valley under the name of Blanc-Fumé where it produces Pouilly-Fumé, Sancerre and Quincy. It has a steely aroma and can make excellent dry, crisp fruity wines. Not

Sauvignon Blanc

perhaps in the same class as the Chardonnay or Rhine Riesling it nevertheless, at its best, produces wines of quality and style. In the 1960s it emerged in California under the name of Fumé Blanc as a crisp, clean and dry wine and has proved extremely popular.

Sémillon A thin-skinned white grape planted in the Graves and Sauternes districts of Bordeaux. It is often used for blending with the Sauvignon Blanc. When visited under humid and warm conditions by the fungus known as *botrytis cinerea* ('noble rot') it rots and

Sémillon

shrivels, its water content is reduced, the sugar content increases proportionally and the grape, when blended with similarly afflicted Sauvignon Blanc and Muscadelle berries, yields the rich sweet dessert wines of which Château d'Yquem is the most renowned. The intense flavour of these wines is almost impossible to describe – one reaches for words like 'nectar' and 'ambrosia' and perhaps finds even these inadequate.

Sylvaner The Sylvaner grape is grown in Alsace, Germany and Austria and it has a mild, soft, fresh and frequently fruity quality. As always, a great deal depends on where the wine is made but the grapes are noted for their low acid content. It has been called, unjustly, the poor man's Riesling.

Sylvaner

Syrah (or **Sirah**) The superb grape which produces red Hermitage made in the town of Tain-l'Hermitage about 50 miles south of Lyon. There is a tradition that the grape was originally brought back to the Rhône from Shiraz in Persia by a homecoming Crusader. Deep in colour, heavy in perfume, strong in tannin, the Syrah is an international grape which makes big robust wines in several other countries. In South Africa it is known as the Shiraz; in Australia, Hermitage. The Californian Petite Sirah has the aroma of blackcurrants almost identical to the Rhône Syrah and

Syrah

the intense black colour but it is not a true Syrah; experts in California are not agreed on its provenance – some say it stems from a grafted variety of Syrah, others that it is a descendant of the Rhône variety called Duriff. 'Petite' it certainly isn't – 'Giant' might be a better adjective.

Trebbiano The most widely planted white wine grape in Italy where it produces such wines as Orvieto and Soave. In France, under the name of Ugni Blanc, it produces the Provençal wine of Cassis and, as St Emilion, it is widely grown in the Cognac region.

Zinfandel The second most widely planted red-wine grape in California. In Italy it is known as the Primitivo di Gioia after a town in the heel of Italy. There it produces a thick, heavy-bodied red wine used in blending. Zinfandel is also grown in Hungary and Yugoslavia. It is a flexible vine which, depending on where it is planted, can produce light and fruity wines or dark wines heavy in tannin which take years to mature in the bottle.

The Making of Wine

If the grape or the blend of grapes determines the basic character of a wine there are many other variables which make one wine different from another. The ground, for instance, in which the vines are planted. If the soil is over-rich in nutrients the vine is apt to produce far too many grapes of indifferent quality. Go to the Upper Douro valley in northern Portugal and there on the steep hillsides it looks as if the vines are planted in a bedrock of slate. The very best vines of Bordeaux often seem to be struggling to survive in barren gravel and the terrain of Burgundy looks endowed more with pebbles and stones than anything else. Vines seem to thrive best in soil which forces them to send their roots down to a great depth, for there the roots can absorb trace elements from the soil which ultimately condition the flavour of the grape. This is particularly valuable in regions where at certain times of the year there is comparatively little rainfall. The finest wines come from vines planted in well-drained vineyards where there is an excess of quartz, slate or chalk.

Climate also plays a major part. Vines are at their best in temperate regions where they can enjoy a winter of cool hibernation and a long hot summer. Heavy rainfall makes juicy grapes; too little rain and the grapes lack juice and yield an unwanted excess of tannin. In some countries, such as Argentina, the vines have to be artificially irrigated, and this too affects the quality of the wine. Too much sun and the grapes become baked; too little and they will fail to ripen properly and produce enough sugar – the resultant wine will be thin, acid and low in alcoholic strength.

The age of the vine is another important factor. Vines take years to reach their peak and then as they age the quantity of the harvest – and eventually the quality – begins to diminish.

Finally, the ways in which the vines are tended (viticulture) and the wine made (vinification) have the most important influence of all. Just as there are good cooks and poor ones, so there are good and bad wine-makers. Like any other product, wine can be made superbly well or indifferently.

When only the finest grapes of the finest years are selected and infinite care is taken in their fermentation and maturing then we have the best and most classic wines: the Grandes Marques of Champagne, the aristocrats of Burgundy and Bordeaux.

Sadly, few of us can afford such wines. The millions of gallons made in wineries all over the world are the product of a compromise between what we would like to drink and what we are prepared to pay. But excellent modern vinification techniques can work wonders and there is no doubt that the quality of ordinary inexpensive wine has improved remarkably in recent years.

We needn't go deeply into the chemical changes that occur when grape juice is turned into wine. The methods of vinification may vary from region to region but the life-cycle of the vine is the same all over the northern hemisphere. The vines usually produce their flower buds sometime between May and June, depending on how far north they are planted. This is an anxious time; a night frost may nip the bud on the vine, a hailstorm may destroy all hopes of a harvest. Then the vine flowers, a period which may last up to a fortnight. Gradually the grapes form from the flowers and begin to fill out.

It will take about 100 days from the formation of flower buds until the grapes are ready to be picked. During that time all manner of disasters may strike – high winds, a sudden storm, a late frost, too much or too little rain, an excess of humidity. The fragile vines have to be sprayed to afford them protection from pest and rot and there is always the anxiety, particularly in northern climes, that there will not be enough sun at the critical late-summer period to ripen the grapes and increase their sugar content.

OPPOSITE AND LEFT *Gathering the grapes in France. Despite modernization in many areas of wine production, grapes are still generally harvested by hand. The mallet enables the pickers to pack a greater number of grapes in each basket.*

Then comes the moment when the grower, with one eye on the sky and the other on his vines, decides that the grapes are ready. Most grapes in Europe are still picked by hand. Bands of migrant workers, students and local villagers, work from dawn to dusk to strip the vines. As soon as the grapes are picked they are taken to the winery where they are pressed or crushed and the juice is run off into a fermenting vessel. The old days when the grapes were trod in wooden vats until the juice flowed went out with the arrival of mechanical power. Today the grapes are crushed in a giant version of the old-fashioned kitchen mincer designed so that, while the skins are crushed, the pips remain whole.

Whether the skins are yellow or red, the juice itself is always a cidery-yellow colour. White wine is generally made from white grapes and red wine from red or black grapes. The skins of the red grapes are fermented with the juice to give the wine its characteristic colour. If pink wine is being made then the skins are allowed to remain in contact with the juice only until the required tinge has been achieved. For white wine the skins are removed from the must, or grape juice, before fermentation.

Fermentation, the process of converting the sugar of the grape into alcohol and carbon dioxide, would, if the grapes were left on their own, occur quite naturally. There are wine yeasts present on the grape skins which will begin the process of breaking down the grapes. Exactly the same thing would happen if you left a bucketful of raspberries lying in a warm place. When the yeasts have finished their job the vinegar bacteria would, if allowed, take over and gradually turn the alcohol into acetic acid.

So to inhibit the action of the wine yeasts sulphur dioxide is added to the grape-must. If too much is added at this stage or when the wine has been made it will have a sulphury taste about it in the bottle. If adding sulphur dioxide to wine sounds like modern adulteration let me say that the practice has been going on for many generations. In fruit-growing areas sulphur dioxide is added to soft fruit on its journey to the jam factory to preserve it from microbe and bacterial attack. Properly done, it leaves no taste behind. The Campden tablets which home wine-makers use are sulphur-based and perform the same function.

Today, more and more wine-makers eliminate the natural yeasts on the skins and add pure cultures of selected wine yeasts to the grape juice. This provides greater control over the quality of the wine that will be produced. The grape juice is then fermented in a variety of casks and vats. They may be made of wood, concrete, stainless steel or glass fibre, but the action that occurs is always the same: sugar is transformed into alcohol.

How quickly this happens and how much conversion occurs is these days automatically controlled. In northern Europe it may be necessary artificially to raise the temperature of the grape juice to induce fermentation; in hotter climes it may be essential to cool the juice to prevent too hasty a fermentation.

Once the fermentation begins a great deal of natural heat is generated and if the temperature in the vat rises too high and too quickly the yeasts will be unable to do their work. So temperature control is all-important. Equally important is the equation which converts the grape sugar into alcohol. If all the sugar is converted during fermentation then a very dry (and strong) wine is created. If you halt the process of fermentation before all the sugar has been converted to alcohol, your wine will be sweeter.

There are other ways of making wine sweet. You can leave the grapes on the vine to soak up every scrap of sunshine so that they become rich in concen-

German law requires that each grade of wine contains a specified amount of sugar. Here, in the Gau-Bickelheim laboratory in the Rheinhessen, the must is being measured for its sugar content.

trated sugar or you can dry the grapes, like sultanas or raisins, in the sun to achieve the same effect. The outstanding naturally sweet wines of Europe are made from over-ripe grapes, some of which may not be picked until the end of the year. Indeed in Germany they even have a name, Christwein, for the sweet wine whose grapes are gathered on Christmas Day.

There are occasions when sugar has to be added to the grape juice before fermenting. This process, called chaptalization in France, after Napoleon's Minister of Agriculture, M. Chaptal, is not intended to make sweet wine but to compensate for the lack of sugar in the grapes after a poor and unsunny summer. There is a precedent in the use of honey in earlier times to achieve the same effect – an increase in the alcoholic strength. In most countries the regulations allowing sugar to be added to the must (grape juice) are strict and in Germany no sugaring is permitted in top quality wines.

Light wines vary in alcoholic strength from as little as 8.5 per cent of alcohol up to 15 per cent depending on the sugar conversion. If you go to the Midi in France, where a huge lake of very ordinary wine is produced, you will find that the criterion for the sale of a *vin*

THE WINE-MAKING YEAR

Methods of viticulture (tending the vineyards) and vinification (converting the grapes into wine) vary from country to country and region to region. The stages shown below relate generally to Europe and show the year from the busy time of the vintage onwards.

Autumn

SEPTEMBER

In the vineyard Harvesting generally begins in the third week, when the grapes are ripe; if the grapes are picked too early they tend to be inferior in quality, but any delay in the expectation of more sunshine could mean the crop is spoiled by unexpected rain or hailstorms.

In the winery After the final racking casks containing last autumn's vintage, now one-year-old, are tightly sealed and turned on their sides for storage.

OCTOBER

In the vineyard The vintage lasts 2 to 3 weeks and the pickers may have to go through the vineyard more than once if the grapes are at different stages of ripeness or if there will be a later harvest of 'noble rot' grapes.

In the winery The new grapes are crushed and pressed (see diagram overleaf) and the juice is run off into fermentation vats. The initial fermentation begins and will in most cases be thermostatically controlled.

NOVEMBER

In the vineyard After the vintage, the leafy shoots are trimmed and the land fertilized and ploughed. The soil is then banked over the vine bases as a protection against winter frosts.

In the winery For red wines, fermentation is rapid for about 5 days. Most reds are run off quite soon to mature in vats or casks; some finer ones will be left to macerate with the skins for up to 3 weeks. White wines generally undergo a longer fermentation, and at a lower temperature.

Winter

DECEMBER

In the vineyard Pruning begins about mid-December and the dead shoots are burnt. On hilly vineyards where the soil has been eroded by rain, earth must be redistributed to provide topsoil.

In the winery Storage casks for new wine must be loosely sealed to allow for the effects of further fermentation.

JANUARY

In the vineyard Training the vines is a vital aspect of pruning, which continues into January. In northerly areas individual vines are trained up single posts to avoid ground frosts. Further south, vines are trained high above the ground in trellises to avoid getting too hot.

In the winery As the new wine throws off more deposit it is racked off the lees to avoid the danger of any off-flavours being imparted to the wine and to renew its store of oxygen. The casks must be topped up with more wine as necessary.

FEBRUARY

In the vineyard Pruned cuttings are taken for grafting on to rootstock. These are planted out in a sandy indoor nursery as a source of new stock to replace the older, less-productive vines. The average productive lifespan of each vine is about 30 years.

In the winery The new wine should be periodically tasted to ensure that the maturation process is going smoothly.

Spring

MARCH

In the vineyard Main pruning ceases as the sap starts to rise in the vines. The vineyard is ploughed, fertilized if necessary, and any banked-up soil is removed from the vine base to allow greater exposure to the benefits of Spring rainfall.

In the winery After the main fermentation, the majority of wines undergo a secondary fermentation in the early Spring. This is caused by bacteria converting malic acid to lactic acid, and reduces the acidity of the wine.

APRIL

In the vineyard Year-old nursery cuttings are planted out and the older vines send out their first shoots which are trained up the lower wires.

In the winery Wooden casks must be continually topped up to prevent the wine oxidizing, since as much as 5 per cent of the wine in these casks can evaporate through the wooden staves in the course of a year.

MAY

In the vineyard Anti-frost precautions get under way to protect the tender young vine shoots. In some vineyards small stoves are distributed among the vines in an effort to raise night temperatures, in others vines are sprayed with water to create a protective layer of ice. Spraying against pests begins.

In the winery Those wines which have undergone a secondary fermentation are racked off their lees into clean vats and casks.

Summer

JUNE

In the vineyard Weather conditions become critical as the vines start to flower. Unsettled weather means uneven flowering and a staggered vintage: wind and rain could remove the pollen impeding the vital pollination process. After the flowering, the best shoots are thinned out to obtain maximum sun.

In the winery More frequent checks are necessary on the wine levels in the vats with the onset of warmer weather and greater danger of evaporation.

JULY

In the vineyard As the first grapes appear, new shoots are pruned back to channel fruitful growth. The vineyard is weeded so that minerals and moisture in the soil are concentrated on the vines.

In the winery Some wines — such as white Bordeaux or Burgundy — can now be bottled, 9 months after the vintage. Prior to bottling, the wine will have been 'fined' at least once to ensure greater clarity. Most wines will remain maturing in the vats for up to 18 months or more.

AUGUST

In the vineyard The grapes begin to ripen and change colour. Spraying ceases and preparations for the vintage begin. Machinery is overhauled and the hostels for the pickers are opened up.

In the winery Empty vats are inspected and sterilized in preparation for the vintage.

THE BASIC PROCESSES OF WINE-MAKING

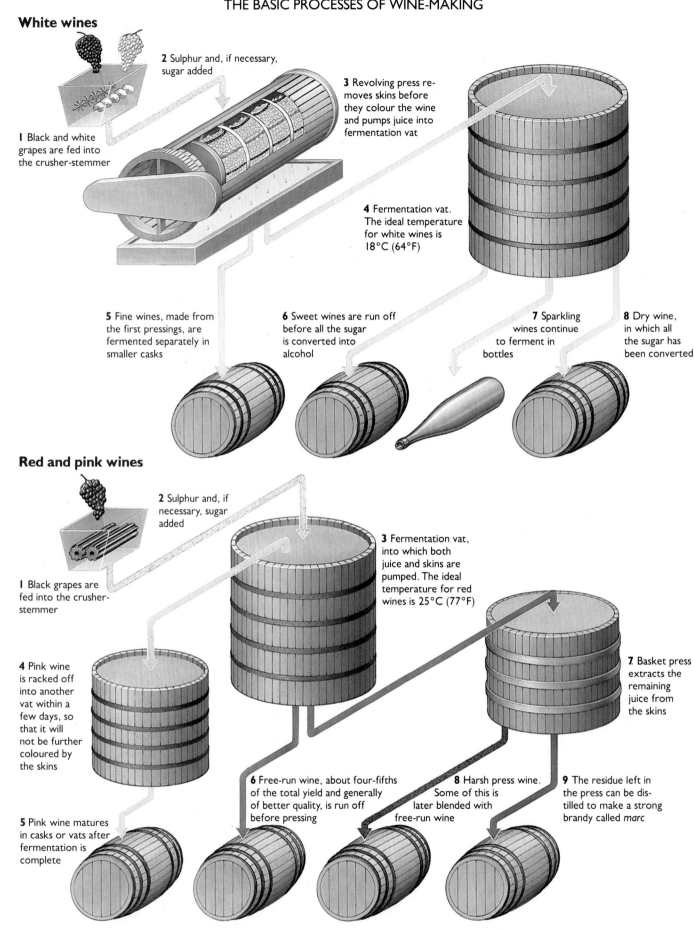

White wines

1 Black and white grapes are fed into the crusher-stemmer

2 Sulphur and, if necessary, sugar added

3 Revolving press removes skins before they colour the wine and pumps juice into fermentation vat

4 Fermentation vat. The ideal temperature for white wines is 18°C (64°F)

5 Fine wines, made from the first pressings, are fermented separately in smaller casks

6 Sweet wines are run off before all the sugar is converted into alcohol

7 Sparkling wines continue to ferment in bottles

8 Dry wine, in which all the sugar has been converted

Red and pink wines

1 Black grapes are fed into the crusher-stemmer

2 Sulphur and, if necessary, sugar added

3 Fermentation vat, into which both juice and skins are pumped. The ideal temperature for red wines is 25°C (77°F)

4 Pink wine is racked off into another vat within a few days, so that it will not be further coloured by the skins

5 Pink wine matures in casks or vats after fermentation is complete

6 Free-run wine, about four-fifths of the total yield and generally of better quality, is run off before pressing

7 Basket press extracts the remaining juice from the skins

8 Harsh press wine. Some of this is later blended with free-run wine

9 The residue left in the press can be distilled to make a strong brandy called *marc*

de table is not its grape of origin but its alcoholic strength. The 'weakest' wines are those made in the Moselle region where the northern summers produce a relatively small amount of sugar. Go further south in France and the strength of a Burgundy goes up to 12 or 13 per cent. White wines from the Loire are usually around 12 per cent while the big red wines of northern Italy and the Rhône vary from 13 to 15 per cent of alcohol by volume.

Once the heaving and bubbling of fermentation is judged to have reached its desired conclusion, the wine is run off into other casks or vats where it will be left to effect a secondary fermentation; the containers can be as small as a barrel or hold thousands of litres. Whatever the size, the solid particles begin to sink to the bottom and are known as 'lees'. When the wine is clear it is 'racked', or pumped, off its lees into empty barrels or containers. Racking may occur more than once. There is fining as well, the process which clears the wine of any suspended particles. Depending on its quality and degree of readiness, the wine may then be blended, filtered and bottled or it may stay in casks for further ageing.

Some wines will be ready for bottling and even consumption a few months after the vintage, others will stay in vats or oak barrels for two or three years or more. Generally speaking red wines heavy with tannin take longer to mature than white but generalizations are misleading. Some of the finest sweet German wines and the Sauternes and Barsacs of France may go on improving in the bottle for a quarter of a century and more, long after most red wines have begun the descent into senility. Wine is a living thing and like all living things it has a youth, a middle-age and then a sad descent into an old and undrinkable age.

Pink wines that have been fermented traditionally contain little tannin and are consequently light and quick to mature. This is because the skins of the red grapes are allowed to lie with the juice only long enough to impart the rosy colour; the wine is then racked off before a deeper red sets in.

The machinery for pressing grapes has evolved over the years. The presses now on display in the Kloster Eberbach Museum in Germany (top) were first used around 1794. Centrifugal separators (bottom) are today used to ensure further purification after the grapes are pressed.

The oak in which a red wine is matured (white wines seldom see wood) will have a profound effect on its eventual flavour. In the great châteaux of Bordeaux new *barriques* (barrels that contain the equivalent of 288 bottles) are bought every year. The new oak adds to the wine's flavour and, some say, enables it to clear more quickly. The old used barrels are sold off to wine-makers with less demanding standards. What goes on in a barrel or a bottle when a wine is maturing is not fully known but it is certainly a process of oxidation which removes harshness, improves the bouquet of the grape used, and gives a wine a chance to reveal all its virtues.

Ninety per cent of the world's wines are drunk young and indeed they are made to be drunk young. Because of the vinification techniques used, it is doubtful that they would improve very much however long they were allowed to age.

The romantic image of wine-making as a rural bacchanalia disappeared with haywains and horses. The electrically operated winery will more likely have a micro-chip processor, a laboratory manned by technicians in white coats and all the paraphernalia of industrial chemistry – computer print-outs, gas chromatography and enough flashing lights to mount a space journey to Mars.

Guesswork is no longer tolerated; stringent quality control, based on carefully laid down formulae, produces wine that aims to be as consistent as possible from one year to another. Mass-marketing does not cherish bountiful vintages one year and a scarcity the next. Even before wine-making begins new techniques are at work. Every wine region has its viticultural research station where expert oenologists are constantly searching for new disease-resistant, vigorous and highly productive vines. The modern hybrids (like the garden pea developed for freezing or the apple bred for its colour and long shelf-life) are not necessarily the vines which are going to produce the greatest wine in the world.

The process for making sparkling wines is initially the same as that for still wines. Sparkling wines can be red

Vineyards must be tended throughout the year, and growers have to cope with the vagaries of climate. Top, vineyards in Ay after the Pinot Noir grapes have been harvested; middle, a vineyard in the Côtes de Provence is made ready for winter; bottom, a Rheingau vineyard under snow – often a time when the vines are pruned.

(although they seldom are), white and pink. Not all wines which sparkle are Champagne thanks to a long legal battle fought by the makers of Champagne. In the EEC countries the name Champagne may only be given to the sparkling wine produced in a delimited area northeast of Paris centred round the three towns of Rheims, Épernay and Ay. The region is so small that it represents only one per cent of the vineyard land of France but it makes the most famous wine in the world. The wine can only be made from certain grapes (Chardonnay, Pinot Noir and Pinot Meunier) by a labour intensive process known as the *méthode champenoise*.

Great care is taken in the production of Champagne. In the gathering of the grapes pains are taken to ensure that no diseased or flawed grapes are used. The pressing of the grapes falls into three stages – only the first pressing is used for the finest Champagnes, the rest goes for the making of lesser wines.

The juice is fermented and the wine made. Then in the spring following the vintage the process of adding the sparkle begins. *Cuvées* or blends of wine are prepared, some from a single year, most from a variety of years, and sugar and yeast are added to induce a secondary fermentation in specially strengthened bottles. This secondary fermentation produces additional alcoholic strength and bubbles of carbon dioxide. There are further ministrations including the addition of a *dosage* to fix the dryness or sweetness of the Champagne. The *dosage* (sugar syrup in old wine) is added even to the driest of Champagnes; otherwise they would be too austere for even the

Making Champagne. The traditional wooden press for Champagne (top) is called a maie. *During the secondary fermentation (see page 118) sediment forms in the bottles. This is removed by a two-stage process,* remuage *(middle) and* dégorgement *(bottom).* Remuage *is said to have been discovered in the early nineteenth century by the widow Cliquot, head of the Champagne firm which still bears her husband's name. She hit on the idea of placing the bottles in specially angled* pupitres *or racks so that a daily shaking and turning gradually moved the sediment down towards the cork. For the* dégorgement, *a skilled worker then eased out the cork – releasing only the small amount of wine which harboured the sediment. Nowadays nearly all firms freeze the bottle neck so that the sediment is contained in a small plug of ice which can be expelled with the minimum loss of wine. Afterwards the bottle is topped up with its appropriate* dosage *and given its second and final cork.*

most sophisticated palate. The *dosage* varies from one-and-a-half per cent (Brut) up to five per cent or more for the dessert Champagnes.

The finest vintage Champagnes are kept in the cellars for up to nine years. Even the youngest may not be sold until they have been in bottle for one year, which makes the wine a minimum of 18 months old. The Champagne process is expensive so the wine will always remain one for special occasions.

Every country which makes still wine also produces sparkling wine. Sometimes the classic *méthode champenoise* is followed but more frequently the fermentation takes place not in a bottle but in a sealed vat (*cuve close*), a method invented by a Frenchman called Charmat. Excellent sparkling wines are made in the Loire district of France, in Italy (where it is called Asti Spumante), in Spain and in Germany (called Sekt). The long-established Champagne house of Moët et Chandon planted a vineyard in the Napa Valley in

Some of the thousands of casks which lie maturing in the red-tiled lodges of Vila Nova de Gaia near the mouth of the river Douro. At least two-thirds of the total stock of port in the lodges is stored in wood but vintage port will spend most of its life maturing in the bottle.

To make Cognac, wine is twice heated in a pot still as shown here; the brandy elements are released in the steam and condensed by cooling. The heart of the distillate, the raw Cognac, is then matured in Limousin oak until it attains a ripe enough age to be blended with other Cognacs to produce the required house style.

California and they are producing what they are careful to call a 'sparkling wine' of very good quality. But it is *not* Champagne.

There are more economic methods of making wine sparkle – injecting it with carbon dioxide, for instance – but however the sparkle is introduced, the quality of the wine will depend almost entirely on the grapes used and the excellence of the base wine. A poor wine makes a poor sparkler.

Fortified wines – sherry, port,

Madeira, Marsala and vermouth – are those to which alcohol has been added either to stop the fermentation and retain the sweetness of the grape or to give the wine a bigger kick.

Like Champagne, sherry is what we might call a 'made' wine and like Champagne its name is legally protected. Sherry is only made in a delimited area round the city of Jerez in the southwest of Spain. The wines, made mainly from the white Palomino grape, are aged in a system peculiar to

Jerez known as the *solera*. The bone-dry young oloroso and fino wines are in effect sent to school with older wines which 'educate' them over the years, lending them elegance and refinement. As the mature wines are drawn off, new wines are added so that in a molecular sense some of the wine drawn off may be very old indeed. In one *bodega* (a warehouse) I was offered a sip from a barrel which had contained wine since 1586, two years *before* the Armada sailed for England. This *solera* ageing continually refreshes the older wines and eventually produces a sherry of remarkable consistency. Sherries have different strengths (most range from 15–22 per cent) and many different styles, one frequently, and imperceptibly, merging into another (see pages 67–9).

Montilla is a sherry-like wine, made to the south of Cordoba, which is so strong in natural alcohol (up to 21 per cent in the olorosos) that it seldom has to be fortified. It is becoming popular as a lower-priced substitute for sherry.

Port, traditionally the Englishman's drink, is made from grapes grown in the Upper Douro valley in Portugal. The fermentation is arrested early in the process of wine-making by the addition of grape brandy which stuns the activity of the yeasts. In the spring following the vintage, the wine-brandy blend (one-fifth spirit, four-fifths wine) is taken down to the town of Vila Nova da Gaia, where it lies in oak casks to mature over the years. It will then be blended; younger wines with older, sweeter with drier, good with better, to produce the particular styles associated with the port-maker concerned. As the wines age they turn from purple to ruby and eventually they become a tawny colour. The youngest port is known as Ruby; the really distinguished ports are those which have been selected from the years of great distinction.

Not every year is considered outstanding enough for the making of vintage port and such a wine may lie up to 15 years in the bottle before it is considered to have reached a reasonable degree of perfection. Many ports continue to improve for a long time after that; as they improve, a sediment or deposit forms in the bottle. This means that the port must almost always be decanted (see page 45) before drinking. Becoming increasingly popular is LBV port – Late Bottled Vintage. This is a port of a single year, although not necessarily a great year. Unlike vintage port which is bottled between its second and third year, it lies in wood until it is between four and six years old and is ready for drinking as soon as it is bottled. It is a lighter wine than vintage port but the fact that almost all of its natural sediment has settled and remained in the barrel means that there is no crust, or deposit, in the bottle. LBV is therefore much easier to serve in these days when few people have a cellar let alone a faithful butler to fiddle about with candles and decanters. It is what you might call a 'convenience' vintage port.

Crusted port derives its name from the sediment which accumulates in the bottle. This is a blend of fine wines, not all of the same year, which has been allowed to mature in bottle for several years.

White port, made from white grapes, is becoming fashionable as a medium or dry apéritif but modern marketing is confounded by the old saw: 'Port has two duties – the first to be red and the second to be drunk'. Port-style fortified wines are made in many countries and some of them achieve great heights; many are very sweet and very horrid.

Madeira, made on the Portuguese island of that name, has its fermentation arrested by the addition of brandy. It is then aged in a *solera* system similar to that used in Jerez. The wines derive their remarkable caramel flavour from prolonged exposure to high temperatures in special rooms called *estufas*. The driest Madeiras are known as Sercial; Bual is sweeter, Malmsey is sweetest of all. Madeira is without any doubt the longest-lived wine in the world.

There are other fortified wines which are less easily obtainable. Pineau de Charentes (grape juice and Cognac) is a fruity French apéritif which is frequently used to fill a scooped out melon; Moscato (wine plus spirit) is made in various parts of Italy; in Roussillon in southern France there is a big trade in 'natural sweet wines' (*vins doux naturels*) which are Muscatel wines fortified with brandy; Malaga on the south coast of Spain also produces a rich wine fortified with brandy.

Vermouths derive their name from the German word for wormwood: *wermut*. These are wine-based apéritifs fortified with spirit and various herbs and spices, among them hyssop, coriander, cloves, camomile, orange peel, quinine, juniper, aloes, cardomum, star anise, ginger, gentian, allspice, horehound and calamus root. The main ingredient is *artemisia absinthium* or wormwood.

Only slightly stronger than table wines, these aromatized concoctions may justifiably be considered the most ancient of all alcoholic drinks, for mixing wines with spices dates back to Greek and Egyptian times. The most highly renowned vermouths are those of France and Italy and the vermouth of Chambéry in France is considered to be amongst the finest. Vermouth comes extra dry, dry or sweet and in three colours: red, white and pink.

When it comes to drinks distilled from the grape then the two greatest are Cognac and Armagnac. Just as the majority of sparkling wines made in various parts of the vine-growing world are not Champagne so not all brandies are as distinguished as Cognac or Armagnac, both of which are distilled and matured under strict control in delimited areas of southwestern France. Although Armagnac is produced from the same grapes as Cognac it has a very different aroma and flavour. It is heavier and more pungent than Cognac and is marketed in a flat long-necked flagon known as a *basquaise*.

Cognac is a brandy twice distilled, as malt whisky is, in a pot still. The wines from which the brandy is made are extremely thin and acid and the art of distillation is later enhanced by the judicious ageing and blending of diverse brandies in oak. The big Cognac houses – Martell, Hennessy, Courvoisier, Rémy Martin, Delamain, Hine – all make different styles and qualities of Cognac which are distinguished by stars and initials. In the finest blends there is a high proportion of old Cognac; the best Cognacs, alas, cost the most money.

OPPOSITE *Red and white vermouth. Vermouth is often made from inferior wine which would otherwise end up as industrial alcohol. But blended with spirits, sugar syrup, herbs and flavourings it makes a pleasant apéritif. Vermouth also forms the base for all sorts of mischievous cocktails, many of them unnecessarily lethal and anaesthetic.*

A Guide to Taste

How can you tell what a wine is going to taste like *before* you pull the cork? The unhelpful answer is that unless you have tried an identical bottle before, then you won't be able to. Although more and more companies are now giving some indication of dryness or sweetness on the label, these are still relative terms. To some people even a Sauternes may be too dry. The words 'dry red wine' or 'medium-dry white wine' are helpful but most bottles on sale do not give any indication of their flavour or indeed their strength, so it does pay to know something about the wine-producing regions and what sort of wines they are likely to be exporting.

I wish it were easier to describe the taste of wine with some hope of accuracy. But taste is a very subjective sensation; what may be sweet to one palate will be only mildly sweet to another. Over the years, however, an accepted vocabulary of adjectives has arisen which members of the wine trade use among themselves to pinpoint the characteristics of a wine.

A wine may be described as fresh, coarse, fruity, light, spicy, sharp, mellow, cloying, elegant, charming, subtle, flat, piquant ... there is no end to the words you can employ to give some indication of the appearance, bouquet, condition, quality, balance, depth and finish of a wine.

Perhaps at this stage it might be helpful to try and define what experts mean when they talk about the aroma of a wine or its bouquet. The aroma is the characteristic fragrance or scent of the grape; how you perceive that fragrance is a highly subjective process. If you find the Sémillon fig-like or the Traminer spicy, then that is an excellent way of remembering it. The bouquet is the smell of the wine itself derived from the distinctive aroma of the grape or blend of grapes used and the physical changes which have taken place during vinification and maturing.

Unfortunately there is a painful tendency among those who write about wine to be carried away by the mellifluousness of their own prose. Sometimes when handled by an enthusiast the magic works. Here's the late André Simon recalling an 1875 Château Margaux: 'It was simply gorgeous! The most glorious sunset that ever fired the West! The bouquet clean, sweet, searching and wholly admirable. Its body free from fat and muscular enormities; attenuated; all in tracings, but wiry, crisp, lithe and lively. A beauty.'

At other times it all sounds a bit

LEFT *Tasting in the cellars of a winery in California, the state which produces 70% of America's output.*

'*It's a naïve domestic Burgundy without any breeding, but I think you'll be amused by its presumption.*'

This cartoon by the late James Thurber deflated a whole generation of wine snobs in the late 1930s and still gives pleasure today.

soppy. It was in these words that the literary wine-lover Maurice Healy described not the elixir of life but a glass of 1889 Burgundy, a Volnay which obviously wasn't too bad: 'I took one sip; I closed my eyes, and every beautiful thing that I had ever known crowded into my memory. In the old fairy tales the prince drinks a magic potion, or looks into a magic crystal, and all the secrets of the earth are revealed to him. I have experienced that miracle. The song of armies sweeping into battle, the roar of the waves upon a rocky shore, the glint of sunshine after rain on the leaves of a forest, the depths of the church organ, the voices of children singing hymns, all these and a hundred other things seemed to be blended into one magnificence.'

So you see what a glass of wine can do to you if you aren't careful! If you think a wine has charm and poise, is moist and spring-like, rather self-satisfied and smug, engagingly youthful, young but full of promise, flinty and hard, big, soft and winsome, then you are perfectly entitled to say so but if someone pulls your leg about it don't be surprised.

If you wish you can talk about wine as if it were a bunch of flowers (fragrant, heavily perfumed); a packet of razor blades (sharp, steely); a navvy (robust, strong, powerful, zestful); a troupe of acrobats (elegant, well-balanced, dazzling); a successful industrialist (rich, distinguished); a young girl (immature but giving promise of pleasure to come); Brighton beach (clean and pebbly); even a potato (earthy). And if you find that helpful then help yourself.

If a wine smells to you of privet, roses, redcurrants, cedar, almonds, vanilla, geraniums, peardrops, pepper or mushrooms then you are not in a minority – such flavours are quite commonly observed by wine experts. And if the wine tastes awful don't be afraid to say so. Wines go through bad periods just as humans do; if a wine is over-sulphured and thoroughly obnoxious in other ways then don't drink it. Wine is for pleasure.

Red Wines It is not easy to classify red wines which vary from the light and dry to the heavy, full-bodied, fruity and robust. There are few sweet red wines. It would not be unfair to say that all the serious wine-makers of the world judge their red wines by the best of those produced in Burgundy and Bordeaux.

In California one of the most talented cellar-masters arranged a tasting of his red wines for me and he paired each of them with what he considered to be the best and most relevant imported French red wine so that I could compare how successfully he had made his 'clarets' and 'burgundies'. I appreciated his modesty but felt it was misplaced. The red wines of countries outside Europe have more than come of age and they should be judged not by the standards of the Médoc or the Côte d'Or but as a product of their own climate, soil and environment. However the temptation will always remain on encountering a really first-class red wine from the Napa Valley in California or the Hunter Valley in Australia to compare it to the best – and undoubtedly the *very* best come from France.

White Wines It is often said that the best white wines in the world come from Germany and that it takes the northern sun to make the most of a great grape like the Riesling but to my mind white Burgundies and the white wines of the Loire valley, the Mosel and Bordeaux are equally outstanding. White wines are even more striking in their diversity than red wines. They can vary from the light bone-dry wine made from the Sylvaner grape, to the crisp Chablis-like wines made from the Chardonnay, the dry Muscadet and Chenin Blanc, and on through a whole spectrum of weight and flavour to the heaviest and sweetest wines of all.

Pink Wines Like white wine, pink may be still or sparkling, dry or sweet, but it is never full or heavy. The principal grapes used to make pink wines are the Cabernet Franc, Pinot Noir, Clairette, Grenache, Gamay and Groslot. Pink is something of a misleading adjective because the wines can vary from the light-beige tone of an onion skin (the French call these wines *pelure d'oignon*) through pale grey to deepest pink. The pink wines of Portugal, Spain, the Jura, Arbois, Anjou and Saumur are well known; even Germany has its pink Schiller wine made in Baden of red and white grapes.

OPPOSITE *This table provides a broad outline of the 'taste' of selected wines from various countries. Taste is, of course, subjective – a wine which some would find medium-sweet would seem very sweet to others. The taste will also vary according to the vineyard of origin of a particular kind of wine.*

A ROUGH GUIDE TO TASTE

The relative qualities of a wine — sweet or dry, light or full — depend on many factors such as climate, the vineyard where the grapes grow, length of fermentation etc. For this reason some wines — such as Vouvray and Chianti — appear in a number of categories. This is only a brief general guide, and should be used as a starting point for your own tasting. Pink wines are not included: most are dry or medium dry.

WHITE WINES	France	Germany	Italy	Spain & Portugal	Others

Bone dry	Alsace Riesling
	Alsace Silvaner
	Anjou
	Chablis
	Muscadet
	Pouilly Blanc Fumé
	Sancerre
	Saumur
		Franken wines
		Ruländer
		Trocken wines of
		    Riesling and
		    Sylvaner
			Trebbiano
			Verdicchio
			Vernaccia
				Dão (P)
				Minho (P)
				Rioja (Sp)
				Valdepeñas (Sp)
					Chardonnay
					Chenin Blanc
					Riesling
					Sauvignon
					Steen

Dry to medium-dry	Bergerac Entre Deux Mers Gewürztraminer Graves Mâcon Blanc Meursault Muscat d'Alsace Pouilly Fuissé Sancerre Sauvignon Blanc Vouvray	Liebfraumilch Mosel Riesling Spätlese wines Sylvaner	Castelli Romani Corvo Bianco Frascati Orvieto Rubesco di Torgiano Soave Trebbiano	Rioja (Sp) Valdepeñas (Sp) Vinho Verde (P)	Chardonnay Chenin Blanc Riesling Sauvignon Steen
Medium-sweet	Coteaux du Layon Gewürztraminer Hermitage Monbazillac Tokay d'Alsace Vouvray	Auslese wines Kabinett wines Liebfraumilch Niersteiner Piesporter Spätlese wines	Abboccato wines Amabile wines Frascati Malvasia Orvieto	Vinho Verde (P)	Muscat Sémillon Steen Wälsch Riesling
Sweet	Barsac Bonnezeaux Cérons Sauternes	Auslese wines Beerenauslese wines	Asti Spumante Muscato wines	Málaga (Sp)	Muscat Tokay
Very sweet	Barsac Sauternes	Eiswein Trockenbeeren- auslese wines	Passito	Priorato (Sp) Moscatel (P)	Tokay

RED WINES	France	Germany	Italy	Spain & Portugal	Others

Light	Beaujolais
	Bergerac
	Côtes du Rhône
	Hautes Côtes de
	    Beaune
	Gamay
	Mâcon Rouge
	Minervois
		German wines are
		predominantly
		white; most of the
		red wines produced
		there are quite light.
			Bardolino
			Castelli Romani
			Chianti
			Merlot
			Valpolicella
				Dão (P)
				Rioja Clarete (Sp)
				Valdepeñas (Sp)
					Cabernet
					    Sauvignon
					Gamay Noir
					Petit Sirah
					Pinotage
					Roodeberg

Medium	Beaune Beaujolais Villages Chinon Côtes du Rhône Graves Margaux Médoc St Julien		Barbaresco Barbera Chianti Chianti Classico Nebbiolo Sangiovese Valpolicella	Navarra (Sp) Rioja (Sp) Valdepeñas (Sp)	Cabernet Franc Cabernet Sauvignon Grenache Pinot Noir Shiraz

Full-bodied	Bordeaux (best
	    growths)
	Burgundy
	Côte Rôtie
	Hermitage
	Rousillon
	St Emilion
	St Estèphe
			Amarone
			Barolo
			Chianti Classico
				Penedes (Sp)
				Rioja (Sp)
					Cabernet
					    Sauvignon
					Pinot Noir
					Shiraz
					Zinfandel

The Rituals

One of the finest meals I had recently was in a hilltop village in the Languedoc to the east of Narbonne. It was a lunch served without pretension and we ate off paper tablecloths – terrines and pâtés, *saucissons*, roast quail, salad, fruit and cheese. With it we drank a red gutsy Corbières wine from tumblers It was a glorious feast eaten in shirt sleeves with no formality.

The following week I dined in the medieval Hall of a livery company in the City of London. Vintage wines, elaborate food, glittering silver, black ties. There were no rituals at the alfresco meal in France, there weren't even labels on the bottles, but it was fun and enjoyable. The dinner was just the

OPPOSITE *While many of the rituals adopted in serving wines are pretentious and unnecessary, most white and pink wines do taste better when chilled.* BELOW *Some common glass shapes. From left to right: Paris goblet, standard tulip, Cognac glass, Champagne flûte, traditional hock and Alsace glass and sherry copita.*

opposite; an occasion for speech-making, ceremony and tradition. I've forgotten what we ate and drank, and only remember the relief of finally escaping from the table into the fresh air.

I'm not decrying formal occasions. They no doubt fulfil a deepfelt social need, but food and drink should not be an occasion for boredom. Guests should sit down with anticipation and pleasure at your table; if they want to leave as soon as possible then obviously something has gone badly wrong. So here are a few simple hints on how to make things go discreetly right.

There are no hard and fast rules about how much wine to serve. The late André Simon, a Frenchman who chose to live in England, once recalled a lunch which he attended in the Montagne de Reims in 1909 when 24 magnums of Heidsieck Dry Monopole 1892 were set

in front of the 24 guests – and consumed down to the last bubble. Two bottles per person is a bit much even by Edwardian standards, but if you allow only half a bottle for each guest you may well be confronted by the embarrassment of empty glasses halfway through the meal. Allow a bottle per person and relax; have a couple in reserve and feel completely confident. What isn't drunk can always be kept for later use.

And how many glasses can you get out of a bottle? It depends on the size of the glasses and indeed how generously you fill them but as a rule of thumb, an average 72–78cl bottle will yield eight glasses of wine, so if you feel that four glasses is all each of your companions will need, then half a bottle per guest is, if not ample, at least adequate.

I once took a rather special bottle of wine to some acquaintances who had asked us to drop in for a snack lunch.

After a great deal of hunting our host found four ill-assorted glasses. They were about the size of eyebaths and held no more than a generous tablespoonful of wine; one sip and you were empty. No matter what anyone says it really does matter that the glasses you put on the table are at least large enough to contain something more than a mere sample of wine. The clearness of the glass is equally important. In the nineteenth-century when wines, particularly white wines, were made less expertly than they are now they frequently contained particles which nowadays would be removed before bottling. It was fashionable to drink hock out of green glasses so that the eye should not be offended by any floating imperfections. But there is no longer any need for such cosmetic help.

Once I was offered a very fine claret in a coffee mug. 'You won't mind, will you, but we haven't washed up from last night and all the glasses are dirty.' I did mind immensely; it was like being offered roast pheasant in a chipped enamel dog's bowl. Whether the wine is red, white or pink its colour should be a joy to behold. Using dark or heavily-cut glass distorts the colour of the wine and lends more importance to the container than its contents. There are many expensive hotels and restaurants which insist on serving wine in cut crystal glasses; to cut glass presupposes that the glass is thick, and apart from the artifice of the glassmaker's skill you might as well be drinking from a moulded jam jar.

If I harp too much on the virtues of clarity in a glass there's a good excuse. Holding a wine up to a clear light to inspect its credentials can tell you much about its age and condition, and is as important as making a subsequent judgment on its smell and taste. Indeed you can almost categorize a wine by its appearance. John Hurley of Hoarwithy in Herefordshire, who writes and lectures on wine, has devised a small checklist which, as a rule of thumb, is most helpful. His colour guide to a wine's age and health reads like this:

A ROUGH COLOUR GUIDE TO THE TASTE OF WINE

White wine		**Red wine**	
Watery white	*young, fresh, light*	Blue/black	*robust, tannic, immature*
Green	*tart, crisp*	Bright red	*thin, light, fresh*
Greeny gold	*more fruit, better balanced*	Brick	*mature, round, ready for drinking*
Gold	*sweet, rich, luscious*	Mahogany	*ageing but still very acceptable*
Brown	*faded, oxidized, flat*	Brown	*old, tired, fruitless*

Over the years a complicated repertoire of wine and spirit glasses has been devised which certainly affords employment to designers and manufacturers. Most of the glasses which are given lavishly as wedding presents remain unused; kept for a 'best' which never presents itself. You don't need masses of different–sized glasses, nor for that matter different–shaped glasses. The ideal glass should have a stem, a generous bowl and an incurving lip to contain whatever aromas will be released from the wine. It should be large enough to hold an adequate amount without having to fill it more than half or two–thirds full. As well as being able to see the colour of the wine you should be able to bask in its bouquet.

The common-sense glass has this stem so that if the wine is cooled or chilled you can hold it without clamping a hot hand round the bowl. The bowl is tulip or onion-shaped so that if you want to swirl the wine around to liven it and release the aromas it won't fly out over your dinner companion's party dress. And ideally the glass should be thin enough so that over-zealously chilled

wine can be warmed to the ideal temperature in the palm of your hand.

Having said that all you need for the enjoyable drinking of any wine is the single ideal glass I must, in fairness, admit that the different wine regions of Europe have over the years evolved traditional glasses which are considered ideal for drinking particular wines.

Go to Anjou, for instance, and you'll find shops selling elegant looking shallow, straight-sided glasses on long stems which would be equally ideal for an ice cream sundae. In Jerez your sherry will be offered in a glass with a tall tulip-shaped bowl known as a *copita*. It has become fashionable in some quarters to serve Burgundy in enormous goblets capable of containing a small shoal of goldfish. Beware of these; some of them can comfortably hold at least a half-bottle of wine and provide the perfect excuse for a wine waiter to whisper audibly in your ear 'Shall I bring another bottle, sir?' Burgundy is drunk very properly in the ordinary Paris goblet holding eight fluid ounces. Alsace, Cognac, Champagne, Mosel and Oporto all have their distinctive

The range of red wines is vast in both colour – including mulberries and browns – and depth. This selection goes from a Rioja on the left to a light, young Beaujolais on the right. Always check that the wine is clear.

glasses but it is no more necessary to acquire regional glasses to serve regional wines than it is to acquire foreign china in which to serve foreign dishes.

Whatever glass you use see that it comes to the table detergent–free and sparkling. Even the slightest residue of washing-up liquid on the surface of a glass can affect the taste of wine. And there's nothing worse than sitting down at a table laid with smeared glasses; even if they are inexpensive, let them sparkle.

All wines are improved by being served at the temperature which best shows off their qualities. Champagnes and sparkling wines should be chilled, not over-iced, before serving. Put them in the refrigerator (not the freezer) for an hour or so to bring them down to a reasonable temperature so that the bouquet is enhanced and your first taste of the wine is both cool and refreshing.

ABOVE *From almost crystal clear to a deep, amber-gold, white wines are as varied in colour as reds. The range shown here is from a Hungarian Tokay, a rich dessert wine, on the left, to a Liebfraumilch on the right.*

LEFT *Early glasses. Left, a Venetian-style glass with a hexagonal bowl set on an elaborate serpentine stem, made in the Netherlands in the seventeenth century. Right, a mid-eighteenth-century glass with a colour twist stem. Both are pretty, but neither is the kind of glass that enhances wine.*

The sweeter the sparkling wine the more chilled it should be. Never put any wine, however indifferent, in a deep-freezer. If you want to chill wine in a hurry (friends arrive on the doorstep announcing imminent marital plans) throw all the ice cubes you have into a bucket of cold water and for added effect put the glasses in the fridge. It's amazing how cool a bottle of wine can become in 10 or 15 minutes. In the depth of a northern winter putting wine on the back porch for an hour or two will probably make it as cold as you want.

But how cold should white or sparkling wine be? The relationship of temperature to taste is a very subjective one, and some white wines taste better than others at cool temperatures. Ambient temperatures also play an important role in deciding how cool or warm a wine should be. On a cold winter's evening you won't want your white wine as cold as you would on a hot summer's day.

Ideally red wine should be warm enough so that its bouquet and flavour can be fully enjoyed. Unless you are bringing it up from a cold cellar or in

from a cold garage, it will almost certainly already be at house temperature and that is ideal. Wine warms in the glass and as it takes on the temperature of the room and becomes what is referred to as *chambré* the aeration noticeably improves it. If you'd spent a long time trapped in a small space you'd expand and feel better once you were released and it's not fanciful to believe that wine, a living thing, has an innate capacity to deliver its best if treated properly.

Just as you shouldn't put white wine in the freezer to accelerate the cooling process, you should never force the warming of a red wine. So don't hold the bottle under a hot tap, or place it next to any kind of fire. That sort of heat is almost equivalent to mulling and it numbs whatever incipient flavours the wine may be about to bestow.

There are some red wines which benefit from being cooled below room temperature. The young Gamay wines from Beaujolais should ideally be served at cellar temperature; this also applies to other young fruity red wines including many from the Loire. Pink or rosé

wines should be cooled as well and all apéritifs benefit from being cooled before serving. This applies just as much to dry sherries and vermouth.

I am one of those insensitive people who puts ice cubes in both red and white wine on very hot days. It dilutes the alcoholic content for a start, which does no harm, and even a red wine can be more refreshing if it is cooled. In Victorian times it was fashionable to dilute German wines with soda water. It is said that Oscar Wilde was sipping a hock and seltzer when the police arrived at the Cadogan Hotel to arrest him. Queen Victoria, who did not approve of Mr Wilde, approved very much of his drink.

If you want some rough guidance on the temperatures at which wines are most frequently enjoyed – and remember that every occasion makes its own demands – then the following figures are not too wildly inaccurate:

Champagne, sparkling and white wines and apéritifs	8–12°C
young red wines	12–15°C
most red wines	15–20°C

When it comes to opening a bottle of wine there is an equally confusing battery of devices from the simple to the technologically complicated. The finest collection of corkscrews I've seen was put together by Brother Timothy, cellarmaster of the Christian Brothers of California, but for opening a bottle you don't need a museum of appliances.

Butterfly levers, two–pronged extractors, counter screws and double spirals all have their attractions and the two-pronged implement is particularly useful in extracting corks that are likely to disintegrate. (With very little practice a cork can be removed *and replaced* without anyone being the wiser, which is why this very versatile device is known as the 'butler's friend'. The discriminating butler, one must assume, might on occasion have replaced his master's Superior Bordeaux with Inferior Plonk.)

I personally don't approve of needle corks powered by bulbs of CO_2. I've seen some messy openings when the cork has shot out under pressure and taken the host by surprise. The other variety of hollow needle down which air can be pumped to raise the cork out of the bottle is ingenious but are these complicated bits of technology really necessary? Like electric carving knives they may make amusing Christmas presents but they tend to lie unused.

I use two devices for opening bottles. The first is called a Lazy Tongs and I bought it in Paris in 1947 for the equivalent of 5p. (Today it costs 40 times as much!) Its spring action makes withdrawing a cork gentle and simple. For recalcitrant corks or those which look as if they might crumble I bring the two-pronged extractor into play; it takes a little practice to use it effectively every time, but its well worth the effort.

If the worst happens and the cork does crumble to pieces then you can always pour the wine through a fine meshed filter to remove the bits and pieces. In dire extremities a cork may even have to be pushed *into* the bottle to get at the wine. Once the cork has been

An armoury of bottle openers. Left: simple corkscrew and two counterscrews; middle: Lazy Tongs and a butterfly lever; right: simple corkscrew, two-pronged 'butler's friend' and its case, and a 'waiter's' all-purpose corkscrew. Of the two simple ones, that on the left has far too little grip to deal with any but the loosest cork; that on the right has a better grip but is too short to deal with a long recalcitrant cork. Choose with care.

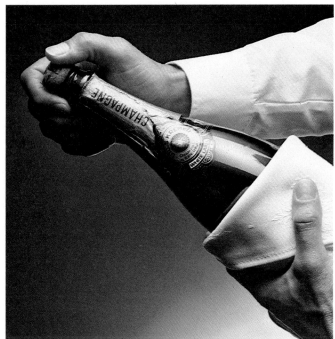

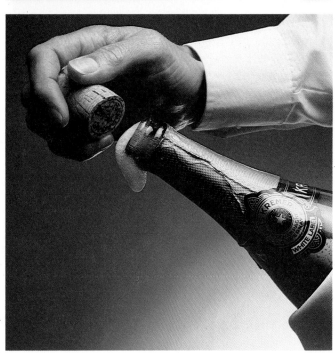

pushed down and out of the neck, hold it in the body of the bottle with whatever is to hand (a toothbrush handle is as good as anything) and pour the wine through a fine strainer into a decanter or jug.

Be sure that before opening a bottle you cut away the foil or plastic capsule so that you are not pouring the wine out over its jagged edges. It is unlikely to harm the wine but at best it looks unsightly and at worst it can deflect the wine on to the table instead of into the glass. It is customary to wrap a napkin round a bottle before opening it. Just as

there is statistically a very remote chance that a syphon of soda may explode there is also a remote chance that any bottle may fracture when the cork is being pulled. For the sake of a cloth or a tea towel it's not worth risking a sliced artery.

When opening a bottle of Champagne or sparkling wine remove the foil, unwire the cork and take care that the bottle is never pointed directly at anyone or any valuable *objet d'art*. The velocity of a flying Champagne cork can give you a very black eye

The first step in opening Champagne is to remove the foil and wire. Then, with one hand round the bottle and the other on the cork, gently rotate the bottle until it releases the cork.

indeed, perhaps worse. But if the cork does fly explosively out of the bottle then you have probably mismanaged things. It should leave the bottle with a gentle and scarcely audible plop.

To open sparkling wine put one hand (right or left; it makes no difference) over the cork and with your other hand

rotate the bottle slowly and gently so that it gradually removes itself from the cork. If the wine foams out – and it shouldn't do so if it has been properly chilled and left unshaken – then hold the palm of your hand over the opening until the first rapturous excess of froth has settled back into the neck of the bottle. Always use a cloth when opening Champagne.

Having determined at what temperature to serve the wine, you have to decide whether to pour it straight from the bottle or transfer it into either a decanter or a jug. Here again we are in the midst of conflicting practices. I have always believed that all red wine improves if it is allowed to 'breathe' – either in a decanter or in a glass – before drinking. Exposing wine to the air, even if you just leave it in the opened bottle, gives it that extra bit of resuscitation that an indifferent wine needs desperately and a fine wine merits.

On the other hand many people think that a lot of this accepted convention may merely be ritual which has no effect on the wine at all. Alexis Bespaloff, the well-known American wine writer, recently conducted some clinical tests to determine whether our view on the correct opening and decanting of wine shouldn't be reconsidered. He chose a selection of fine wines and uncorked and decanted them at carefully predetermined times. One he uncorked and served immediately. At blind tastings attended by some of the finest palates in the New World the wine which was aired the least received the highest praise. Bespaloff's researches had been stimulated by M. Emile Peynaud, the internationally famous Bordeaux University oenologist and technical adviser to many famous châteaux of the Gironde, including Lafite. M. Peynaud had observed that claret was only minutely affected by exposure to the air even for periods of several hours. Despite this research I shall continue to let my red wine breathe just as I shall continue to believe that a red sky at night is a shepherd's delight. Old habits die hard and I still have a strong

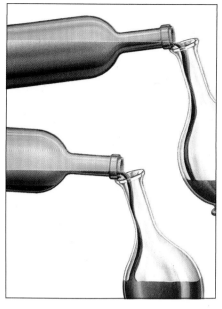

If you do decant wine, keep the bottle as level as possible to ensure that no sediment is transferred, and stop pouring before the sediment, with the last of the wine, reaches the neck of the bottle. Steady the bottle on the decanter and always make sure that the decanter is spotlessly clean.

suspicion that decanting does bring detectable improvements.

One way to expose a wine to the air fairly quickly is to pour it from a height into a jug. I wouldn't recommend that you do this with the elderly product of a great château, but no young red wine is going to be damaged by such aerial gymnastics. Very old wines which have thrown a sediment are always carefully decanted so that the lees remain in the bottle. If you don't decant a wine which has a deposit you run the risk of stirring up the murk and eventually pouring it into someone's glass.

Few of us will be confronted very frequently by old wine so a discussion on the niceties of decanting is perhaps academic. But if you are decanting, hold both bottle and decanter up to the light and stop pouring while the cloudy remnants are still in the bottle. You can always use the dregs for cooking.

White wine does not generally improve by being opened in advance but it always gives the stale air inside the bottle, which sometimes can release an unpleasant smell known as bottle stink, a chance to dissipate. Swilling the wine round in the glass can achieve the same result.

If an open bottle of wine is left to its own devices it will almost certainly turn to vinegar. White wine can be recorked and kept in the fridge without obvious

deterioration for several days. There is a special all-purpose stopper available which can be clamped over Champagne and sparkling-wine bottles to keep the bubbles in and the air out. Ideally wine keeps better out of contact with air, so it's not a bad idea, if you have less than half a bottle left, to pour it into something smaller and recork it. No wine keeps indefinitely; even sherry, particularly fino, begins to fade once the cork is drawn. Fortified wines are best kept in the fridge while red wines may keep for up to a week if properly restoppered.

These days there is an increasing use of plastic stoppers instead of corks. Many sparkling wines, for reasons of economy, are stopped with a 'cork' which has the same shape and flexibility as a champagne cork but which can be mass-produced for a fraction of the price. The function of a plastic cap is identical to the function of the cork: it prevents the entrance of air and the consequent risk of damaging the wine by oxidation. There is, too, an increasing use of screwtops for wines which are meant to be drunk very young.

An all-purpose stopper, designed to prevent Champagne and other sparkling wines going flat.

If red wine is poured accidentally on to a tablecloth or somebody's clothing it can be lifted almost magically by thoroughly neutralizing it with white wine. If no wine is available apply lots of cold water or salt. If wine is spilt on a carpet don't go dashing about looking for a cloth. Grab the nearest piece of absorbent paper (newspapers or paper towels are ideal) and soak up as much as you can as quickly as you can. Rubbing with a cloth only serves to spread the wine to an even wider area – mopping and absorbing is the right thing to do. Salt, which absorbs moisture, is also very effective. White wine when spilt is less of a problem as it tends to leave very little discolouring behind.

If you don't live in a house with a cool constant-temperature cellar then the problem of storing wine can be a cause for concern. Garages and attics can be subject to wide ranges of temperature and the one thing wine doesn't relish is a see-sawing between heat and cold. Wines like to be left in a dark place to mature, preferably one which is cool all the year round. Damp is often an asset; it keeps the corks from drying out and wines have been known to live happily for years in moist cold cellars visited by fungus and bacterial growth.

If you live in a flat at the top of a building where the roof is not well insulated then any wine you have may be exposed to fairly wide ranges of temperature. The best place to keep your wine would be in a dark cupboard as far from a radiator or direct source of heat as possible.

There is general agreement that cooler temperatures are the best for ageing the lighter and less alcoholic wines, warmer for the bigger table wines, and warmer still for fortified wines. Heating a wine is the quickest way to mature it (or ruin it) and both the Greeks and the Romans exposed their wine to the sun to improve it. On the other hand the subtleties of Champagne are only fully revealed after prolonged storage at the relatively low temperature of 10°C.

Perhaps the perfect answer for flat dwellers and those who live in houses over-centrally heated is the Eurocave, a cabinet not unlike an upright freezer which can hold either 100, 140, or 240 bottles at three different temperatures. Sectionalized for the separate storage of white wine, red wine and Champagne the cabinet is expensive but effective.

Always keep your bottles lying on their sides so that the wine is in constant contact with the cork. If left standing for any length of time the cork will dry out and shrivel and your wine will begin to oxidize and evaporate.

Spirits do not continue to improve in the bottle and neither, generally speaking, do sparkling wines or Champagnes which are always sold ready for drinking – if you leave them lying around too long their initial sparkle may well dissipate. As a rule dry white wines are intended to be drunk fairly young and to keep them for any prolonged length of time is unwise. This does not apply to the very sweet wines, the greatest of which can go on improving for decades.

OPPOSITE AND LEFT *Wine can be stored in a variety of ways and places. Always keep bottles on their sides, and try to find a place which has a constant temperature. A cardboard box is perfectly adequate; collapsible wine racks are inexpensive and very portable. If you are really pressed for space, try storing your bottles in a cupboard under the stairs. Bottom right, a rather grander storage setting, in the Veuve Cliquot cellars at Rheims.*

Reading the Bottle

What words can and cannot be printed on a label is rigorously controlled in Britain by various Acts of Parliament (Customs and Excise, Food and Drugs, Weights and Measures, Trade Descriptions) and by regulations and directives set out by the combined authority of the European Economic Community. In addition various judicial decisions have further limited what one may or may not call a wine in Britain.

Take sherry. Sherry was originally produced only in a small area around the little town of Jerez de la Frontera in southwest Spain. Then sherry-type wines came to be made elsewhere: in Cyprus, South Africa, Australia, even in Britain. In 1925 the Sherry Shippers' Association brought an action against an English firm which was marketing a wine called Corona Pale Sherry ('produced in England from the juice of selected foreign grapes').

The evidence to prove that the English sherry was a bogus product associating itself improperly with 'real' sherry was not very efficiently presented and the Sherry Shippers lost their action. They had to wait 36 years before they were able to strike again. In 1961 a group of Champagne producers brought a case in the English courts against a company that was selling a sparkling wine described as Spanish Champagne. Mr Justice Danckwerts ruled in favour of the Frenchmen and prohibited the use of the description 'Spanish Champagne'.

This encouraged the Sherry producers to prepare an action against a group of British firms who were between them selling about 80 per cent of British sherry in the United Kingdom as well as importing 'sherry' from Cyprus, Australia and South Africa. The preparation of the case took three-and-a-half years; the trial lasted 29 days and more than 70 witnesses testified. What the merchants of Jerez objected to was the advertising which frequently suggested that beverages made in Britain had legitimate connections with Jerez. Spanish bullfighters and girls with mantillas were invoked along with Spanish-sounding names like Pedro and Paco to create a spurious Iberian aura. One advertising campaign featured a swarthy hidalgo in a wide-brimmed sombrero and bullfighting outfit praising the excellent qualities of a drink fabricated in a winery in Kingston-upon-Thames.

The verdict was not as clear-cut as it had been in the case of Champagne but it did insist that in future any reference to Sherry, unless it came from Jerez de la Frontera, would have to carry a geographical qualification: 'British' Sherry, 'Cyprus' Sherry and so on. Thus was justice more or less done.

There has always been a temptation, whether in the world of art, stamp-collecting or wine, to pass spurious objects off as genuine. It was to combat fraud and imitation that the French introduced a series of very elaborate wine laws after the First World War. It was a time of hardship when many honest growers found that their own authentic wines were being challenged by inferior wine from other countries and other regions of France, like the Midi, where quantity was more in evidence than quality.

By 1935 the French government had created a system of rules and regulations (called *appellations contrôlées*) which gave official recognition and legal definition to the name a wine was permitted to bear. Violation of the laws, if detected by the Suppression of Fraud Squad, made the offender liable to heavy fines or even imprisonment.

What vines could be planted, how many to the hectare, how the pruning was to be done, how much wine could be produced, the alcoholic strength, the naming of the wine, were all controlled. Wine given the *Appellation d'Origine Contrôlée* (AOC or AC as it's known) had to be able to prove its authenticity with the appropriate documents. It was a system which guaranteed *origin* but not *quality*.

Until 1975 a grower could take advantage of what was known as the *cascade* option whereby if he exceeded his permitted yield he could declassify the wine to a lower category. This has now been replaced by a tighter system which no longer allows surplus wine to be juggled with; anything over the fixed percentage must be made into vinegar or go for distillation.

Most countries followed the example of France and introduced laws to protect their quality wines but they vary from the Teutonic thoroughness of the Germans to the relative laxity of Spain. When the European Economic Community was set up in 1957 it instituted a series of committees which are in constant contact with members of the wine industry.

The Commission has issued a set of rules relating to vineyard size, viticultural and vinification practices, control of minimum prices, imports, exports, bottle sizes, labelling, advertising and quality. But the Commission respects the right of an individual county to make national rules for its own wine. Some countries regulate their quality wine largely by quantity (France is a good example), others by qualitative analysis – and here Germany leads the world. In Germany, for instance, samples of wine from every property are analysed after each vintage and if they are found to be unworthy they are refused authentication. In Bordeaux a classified château receives its appellation from a long tradition of excellence, not on the basis of an annual appraisal of its wine.

Yet all the legislation in the world will not prevent a proliferation of clever marketing and often downright dishonest labelling that may lead you to believe you are buying something better than you are paying for. As recently as October 1979 a massive fraud run by an Italian organized crime syndicate was revealed in Britain. The syndicate had forged Mateus Rosé labels and put them on squat, Mateus-shaped bottles with identical gold capsules. The bottles contained sparkling wine from the Asti district and were offered for sale in Germany, Holland and Britain at keenly competitive prices. Although the shipments were impounded before they were sold the fraud could easily have succeeded.

An even saucier fraud which relied

LEFT *A few of the vast number of branded Liebfraumilch.*

OPPOSITE *A range of fairly common bottle shapes. From left to right : Bordeaux, Burgundy, Chianti* fiasco, *classic German bottle, Champagne magnum and bottle, Alsace flûte and Franconian* bocksbeutel.

BELOW *Of those bottles pictured here, the* fiasco *and* bocksbeutel *are perhaps the most familiar. The others indicate the surprising variety of possible shapes and sizes.*

for its success on the complete inability of 999 out of 1000 people to tell one wine from another was unmasked in the spring of 1980. For two years an enterprising Dutchman had been shipping cheap French wine to the United States via Britain where it was labelled Appellation Contrôlée Pouilly-Fuissé. The wine, which was worth about $1, was selling in the States for between $11 and $12. When the enquiry began it was estimated that a quarter of a million bottles of the bogus Pouilly–Fuissé had been drunk by unsuspecting Americans. The Dutch, equally undiscriminating, have also drunk various fake wines labelled by the busy Dutchman and as the investigations continued it began to look as if millions and millions of bottles of completely misrepresented wine had found their way into shops as far apart as Amsterdam and Los Angeles.

Familiar brand leaders are of course fair game for imitators. If one firm has a success with a Liebfraumilch called Red Monk there is little to stop competitors from inventing Red Priest or Red Nun or Red Cardinal. Liebfraumilch, a mild semi-sweet drink much to the British taste, has no less than 70 brands competing on the UK market, many of them using very similar highly coloured labels. Which one would you choose for instance? Blue Max, Blue Horizon, Blue Danube, Blue Nun? Gold Cap, Goldener Oktober, Gold Label? Red Siegel, Black Knight, Black Tower, Silver Goblet, Silver Horn? Or would you opt for something more religious sounding? St Dominic, St Georg, St Jacob? Or perhaps something more aristocratic out of the Almanach de Gotha: Habsburg, Crown of Crowns, Your Crown, Kron Prinz, Kayserdom, Kaiserinuta or Hockprinz?

I really couldn't advise you and without tasting them all no one else could either. What's in a name?

One thing well worth remembering is that a reputable retailer selling the product of a reputable shipper is some guarantee of quality, but even the most reputable have their off days and their subsequent failures. A consignment of wine bought by an importer on the strength of a sample tasted in London may turn out, when the shipment arrives, to be something very different – occasionally inferior and sometimes completely unacceptable. What happens then is up to the shipper. Perhaps he can refuse to accept it; perhaps he can get the price halved and sell it off as cooking wine. But if he takes it and sells it at full price, how many of his customers will be able to tell the difference? More important, how many experts could go into a witness box and prove beyond a shadow of a doubt that one glass of wine was not the same as another? If you buy a saucer you can see at once if it is chipped or flawed. The palate is less educated than the eye. Is it really a different wine from the one you bought last time? Does it taste *that* bad anyway?

The only true way to determine the value inside a bottle is to buy it, pull the cork and rely on your own reaction.

The shape, size and colour of bottles can vary according to the country of origin and the kind of wine inside. Similarly, the information given on the label is determined by whatever regulations the producing country is subject to. So let's look at these differences country by country, and see just what the information is telling us.

READING A LABEL

Surprisingly, wine labels only came into general use around 1914 — before that they were used on only the finest wines. Since then, the regulations governing the information supplied on each bottle have become more comprehensive in order to ensure reliable quality control. Nowadays, each country of origin has its own set of regulations, and reading the bottle correctly can at times seem somewhat daunting. However, as the following breakdown of 5 wine labels — each selected from a different country of origin — shows, the basic ground rules are simple enough, and, once mastered, do provide a very helpful guide to what you can expect of the bottle you buy.

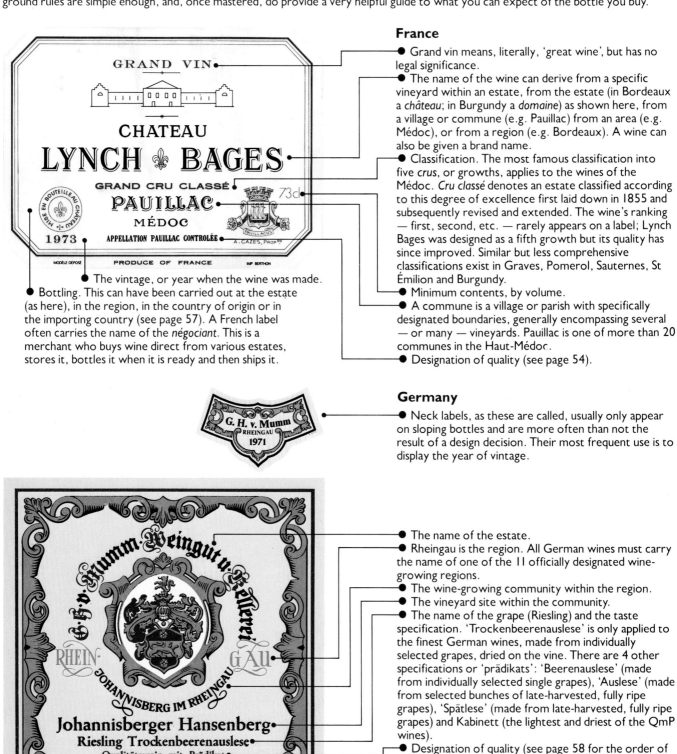

France

● Grand vin means, literally, 'great wine', but has no legal significance.

● The name of the wine can derive from a specific vineyard within an estate, from the estate (in Bordeaux a *château*; in Burgundy a *domaine*) as shown here, from a village or commune (e.g. Pauillac) from an area (e.g. Médoc), or from a region (e.g. Bordeaux). A wine can also be given a brand name.

● Classification. The most famous classification into five *crus*, or growths, applies to the wines of the Médoc. *Cru classé* denotes an estate classified according to this degree of excellence first laid down in 1855 and subsequently revised and extended. The wine's ranking — first, second, etc. — rarely appears on a label; Lynch Bages was designed as a fifth growth but its quality has since improved. Similar but less comprehensive classifications exist in Graves, Pomerol, Sauternes, St Émilion and Burgundy.

● Minimum contents, by volume.

● A commune is a village or parish with specifically designated boundaries, generally encompassing several — or many — vineyards. Pauillac is one of more than 20 communes in the Haut-Médoc.

● Designation of quality (see page 54).

● The vintage, or year when the wine was made.

● Bottling. This can have been carried out at the estate (as here), in the region, in the country of origin or in the importing country (see page 57). A French label often carries the name of the *négociant*. This is a merchant who buys wine direct from various estates, stores it, bottles it when it is ready and then ships it.

Germany

● Neck labels, as these are called, usually only appear on sloping bottles and are more often than not the result of a design decision. Their most frequent use is to display the year of vintage.

● The name of the estate.

● Rheingau is the region. All German wines must carry the name of one of the 11 officially designated wine-growing regions.

● The wine-growing community within the region.

● The vineyard site within the community.

● The name of the grape (Riesling) and the taste specification. 'Trockenbeerenauslese' is only applied to the finest German wines, made from individually selected grapes, dried on the vine. There are 4 other specifications or 'prädikats': 'Beerenauslese' (made from individually selected single grapes), 'Auslese' (made from selected bunches of late-harvested, fully ripe grapes), 'Spätlese' (made from late-harvested, fully ripe grapes) and Kabinett (the lightest and driest of the QmP wines).

● Designation of quality (see page 58 for the order of these designations).

● Amtliche Prüfungsnummer (AP) — the official quality testing number. All QbA and QmP wines must be awarded an AP number as a guarantee that they have been checked for quality.

Italy

● The name of the producing company. Often smaller producers, in Italy and elsewhere, join together in a cooperative to blend, age, bottle and market their wines. In such cases, the name of the cooperative will appear, rather than that of the individual producer.

● The name of the wine. This can be a geographical area, a variety of grape or simply a name chosen by the manufacturers (as here).

● The name of the area. Chianti Classico is named after the Chianti region of Tuscany; Classico specifies that the wine comes from the original centre of the region.

● Designation of quality. Denominazione di Origine Controllata (DOC) ensures that the contents of the bottle correspond to the label's claims.

● This wine has been bottled in the region by the producing company. A label could also say *imbottigliato in zona di produzione* to indicate that it was bottled in the area of origin.

● The per cent of alcohol in the wine, by volume.

● The EEC 'e' (introduced in 1978) signifies that the quantity stated on the label has been checked at source.

● Minimum contents, by volume.

Additional useful information on an Italian label could be the inclusion of a 'Riserva', signifying that the wine has been aged for a statutory period (in this case 'Riserva Ducale' is the registered trademark).

Spain

● Designation of quality. The Spanish Denominacion de Origen (DO) is the equivalent of Italy's DOC, and was introduced in 1970. Only 30 per cent of Spanish wine production is as yet covered by controlling laws but the Rioja quality control is one of the most stringent.

● Vintage.

● The name of the producing company (*bodega*). In Rioja, the *bodega* is as important as, for example, the Champagne houses in France, since each *bodega* has a particular method of blending and ageing.

● Minimum contents, by volume.

● Ollauri is a village near Haro in the Rioja Alta district of the Rioja region.

● Bottling. In Spanish this would read *embotellado en bodega*.

● The name is chosen by the *bodega*. This can be a made-up name, as here, or derived from the region of origin.

California

The name of the producing company. ●
Vintage. ●
The name of the area, in this case Sonoma County, a recently designated area northwest of the more well-established Napa Valley region. ●
The name of the wine, which is — as is often the case with American wines — also the name of the principal grape. ●
Alcoholic content. ●
Bottling. Additional information is given about the number of bottles produced in this vintage. ●
It is a recent innovation to add to the label very specific information about how the wine has been made; this is found primarily on American and Australian labels. ●

Chardonnay

I am very pleased with my 1978 Chardonnay, as it is richer and fuller than my 1977 Chardonnay, being somewhat like my '74 and '76 vintages of this variety.

This wine is produced entirely from Chardonnay grapes grown on several carefully selected vineyards in northern Sonoma county. A total of 61 tons was harvested between Sept. 8 and Sept. 22, at an average sugar content of 23.5° Brix (% by wt.) and a total acidity of 0.79% (% by vol.). After crushing and pressing, the juice was cold fermented to dryness at about 55° F. in stainless steel tanks. Aging occurred in French oak barrels with the wine being bottled in the summer of 1979.

I hope you will enjoy this wine and visit us at the winery.

David A. Mace
Winemaker

DRY CREEK VINEYARD, HEALDSBURG, CALIFORNIA

France

The Bordeaux bottle has a broad shoulder to retain the sediment and a long neck developed to hold the extra long corks used to preserve fine wines as they age. There is a marked indentation or punt in the bottom of the bottle which strengthens it and also forms a reservoir for sediment. Red wine is bottled in green glass; white wine in clear glass. The normal bottle is 75cl rising to the Imperial which contains six litres. This shape of bottle is used for claret-style wines all over the world. In 1980 the 75 members of the *Union des Grand Crus* adopted a new bottle designed exclusively for their use. It is a much darker colour and absorbs 90 per cent of ultra-violet light. A stylized château is engraved on the neck of the bottle to symbolize the great growths of Bordeaux. The first vintage to be bottled in the new style was that of 1977, probably the most disappointing since 1972. It is true for Bordeaux, and all wines, that the smaller the bottle the faster the wine ages. Maturing is caused mainly by oxidation and, relative to the amount of wine, more air is trapped in a half-bottle than, say, a magnum or a six-bottle jeroboam. Thus a half-bottle will be ready for drinking earlier than a bottle.

Red and white Burgundy comes in slope-shouldered bottles – dark green for red wine, olive green for white. Again this is a bottle shape that is found in Italy, Spain and most other wine–producing areas.

Alsace wines appear in green tapering bottles known as flûtes. Many pink wines are found in clear versions of the flûte. In the Loire, too, the bottles taper and are usually made of pale green glass.

Champagne comes in a thick bottle with a special lip to hold the agrafe or crown cork, depending on the technique used in the making of the wine. The bottles are green, 80cl in capacity and specially thickened to withstand up to six times the normal atmospheric pressure.

French wines fall into several categories. The French drink *vin ordinaire*, ordinary everyday table wine with no pretensions of origin, by the litre. *Vin de Pays* is *vin ordinaire* that qualifies for departmental status (as *Vin de Pays du Gard*). Seventy-nine regions of France currently produce named *vin de pays*; the number is subject to change.

The next stage up is *Vin Delimité de Qualité Supérieure* (VDQS) – a wine which conforms to rules and regulations laid down in 1949. The type of grape, the method of vinification and other guidelines are laid down for VDQS wines and these guarantee the method of production if not the actual quality of the wine in the bottle.

Appellation (d'Origine) Contrôlée (AC or AOC) is an even more distinguished wine, one which has been produced according to certain rules administered by the INAO, the *Institut National des Appellations d'Origine*, which also supervises VDQS wines. The type of vines

The main types of wine from each major wine-producing area. (R: red; W: white; P: pink. The table on page 35 provides a general guide to which wines are dry, medium or sweet.)

CHAMPAGNE
Champagne W

ALSACE
Gewürztraminer W
Muscat d'Alsace W
Pinot Blanc W   Pinot Noir W
Riesling W   Silvaner W
Tokay d'Alsace W

LOIRE
Anjou R W P
Bourgeuil R
Chinon R W P
Coteaux du Layon W
Muscadet W
Pouilly Fumé W
Quincy W
Sancerre R W P
Saumur R W P
Savennières W
Touraine R W P
Vouvray W

BOURGOGNE (Burgundy)
Beaujolais R   Beaune R W
Chablis W   Chassagne Montrachet R W
Gevry Chambertin R   Givry R W
Mâcon R W   Meursault R W
Nuits St Georges R W   Pouilly Fuissé W
Puligny Montrachet R W   Volnay R

JURA AND SAVOIE
Arbois R W P   Côtes de Jura R W P
L'Étoile W   Seyssel W

BORDEAUX
Barsac W   Blaye R W
Bourg R W   Cadillac W
Cérons W   Entre deux Mers W
Graves R W   Graves Superieur W
Margaux R   Médoc R
Pauillac R   Pomerol R
St Emilion R   St Estèphe R
St Julien R   Ste Foy Bordeaux R W
Sauternes W

CÔTES DU RHÔNE
Beaumes-de-Venise W
Châteauneuf-du-Pape R W
Côte Rôtie R   Hermitage R W
Lirac R W P   Tavel P

CÔTES DE PROVENCE
Bandol R W P   Cassis R W P

LANGUEDOC-ROUSSILLON
Banyuls W   Corbières R W P
Rivesaltes W

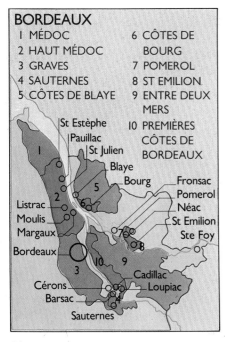

BORDEAUX

1 MÉDOC
2 HAUT MÉDOC
3 GRAVES
4 SAUTERNES
5 CÔTES DE BLAYE
6 CÔTES DE BOURG
7 POMEROL
8 ST EMILION
9 ENTRE DEUX MERS
10 PREMIÈRES CÔTES DE BORDEAUX

St Estèphe
Pauillac
St Julien
Blaye
Bourg
Fronsac
Pomerol
Néac
St Emilion
Ste Foy
Listrac
Moulis
Margaux
Bordeaux
Cadillac
Loupiac
Cérons
Barsac
Sauternes

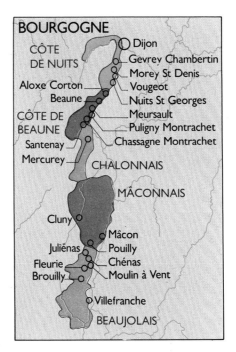

BOURGOGNE

CÔTE DE NUITS
Dijon
Gevrey Chambertin
Morey St Denis
Aloxe Corton
Vougeot
Beaune
Nuits St Georges
CÔTE DE BEAUNE
Meursault
Puligny Montrachet
Santenay
Chassagne Montrachet
Mercurey
CHALONNAIS
MÂCONNAIS
Cluny
Mâcon
Juliénas
Pouilly
Fleurie
Chénas
Brouilly
Moulin à Vent
Villefranche
BEAUJOLAIS

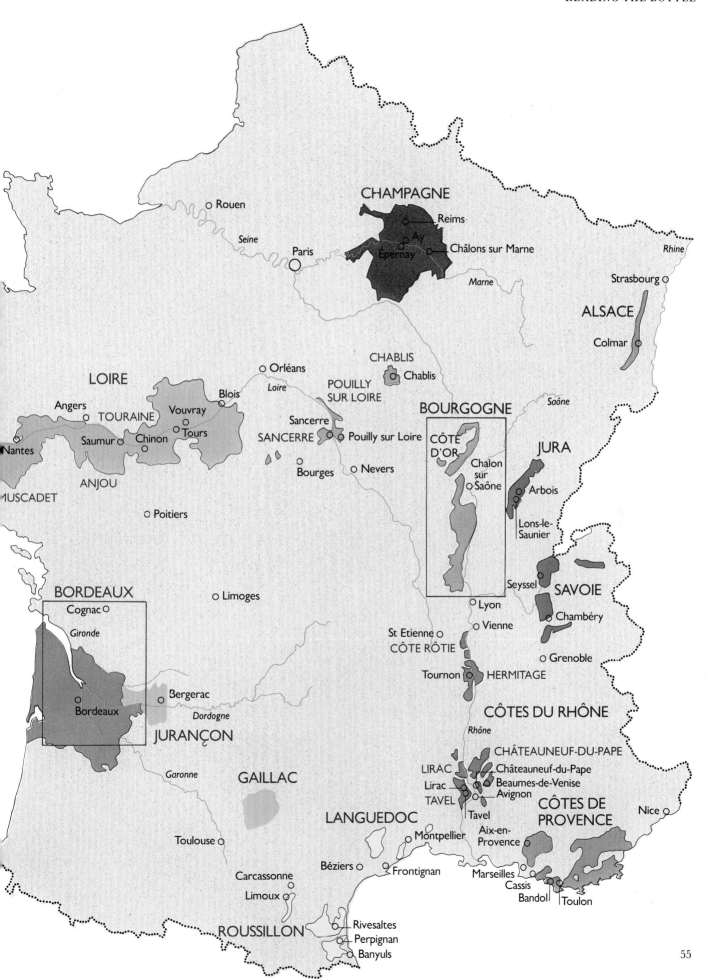

CHAMPAGNE

Rouen

Seine

Reims
Ay
Épernay
Châlons sur Marne

Marne

Paris

Rhine

Strasbourg

ALSACE

Colmar

CHABLIS

Chablis
Chablis

Orléans

Loire

POUILLY
SUR LOIRE

Saône

BOURGOGNE

LOIRE

Angers
Vouvray
TOURAINE
Blois
Saumur   Chinon   Tours
Sancerre
SANCERRE   Pouilly sur Loire

Nantes

MUSCADET

ANJOU

Bourges   Nevers

Poitiers

CÔTE
D'OR

Chalon
sur
Saône

JURA

Arbois

Lons-le-
Saunier

BORDEAUX

Cognac

Gironde

Bordeaux

Bergerac

Dordogne

JURANÇON

Limoges

St Etienne
CÔTE RÔTIE

Tournon   HERMITAGE

Seyssel

SAVOIE

Chambéry

Grenoble

Lyon

Vienne

CÔTES DU RHÔNE

Rhône

CHÂTEAUNEUF-DU-PAPE

Garonne

GAILLAC

LANGUEDOC

Toulouse

Carcassonne

Limoux

Montpellier

Béziers   Frontignan

LIRAC
Lirac
TAVEL
Tavel

Châteauneuf-du-Pape
Beaumes-de-Venise
Avignon

Aix-en-
Provence

Marseilles
Cassis
Bandol   Toulon

CÔTES DE
PROVENCE

Nice

ROUSSILLON

Rivesaltes
Perpignan
Banyuls

APPELLATION CONTRÔLÉE

Although the AC designation (*see page 49*) only guarantees the origin of a wine, informally it is regarded by many as a good guide to a wine's quality. There are many smaller AC areas within the larger ones and, generally speaking, the smaller that area is the better the wine will be. New ACs are awarded when communes or vineyards meet the exacting standards required by the INAO and are then elevated from VDQS status. France was the first country to introduce such legislation; others, such as Italy with its DOC system, have since followed suit.

BORDEAUX
The AC designations in Bordeaux are quite straightforward, and fully two-thirds of the wine made there is good enough to earn the AC guarantee. General regional ACs are Bordeaux, Bordeaux Supérieur (this simply indicates a higher minimum alcohol content), Bordeaux Clairet (or Rosé) and Bordeaux Mousseux.

MÉDOC
Haut Médoc
Listrac
Margaux
Médoc
Moulis
Pauillac
St Estèphe
St Julien

BORDEAUX CÔTES DE CASTILLON
Bordeaux Côtes de Castillon
Bordeaux Supérieur Côtes de Castillon

GRAVES
Cérons
Graves
Graves Supérieur

SAUTERNES
Barsac
Sauternes

ST EMILION AND SURROUNDINGS
Lussac St Emilion
Montagne St Emilion
Parsac St Emilion
Puisseguin St Emilion
Sables St Emilion

St Emilion
St Georges St Emilion

POMEROL
Lalande de Pomerol
Pomerol

CÔTES DE BLAYE
Blaye
Côtes de Blaye
Premières Côtes de Blaye

CANON FRONSAC
Canon Fronsac
Côtes Canon Fronsac
Côtes de Fronsac

CÔTES DE BOURG
Bourg
Bourgeais
Côtes de Bourg

ENTRE DEUX MERS
Cadillac
Premières Côtes de Bordeaux, St Macaire
Entre Deux Mers
Entre Deux Mers Haut Benauge
Graves de Vayres
Loupiac
Ste. Croix du Mont
Ste. Foy Bordeaux

BURGUNDY
Burgundy, or Bourgogne, has more than twice as many ACs as Bordeaux, largely because in the Côte d'Or individual communes as well as all the grands crus are allowed to use their own names as AC designations. Additionally, premiers crus are entitled to add their names to the name of the commune (both in the same size) to form an AC. You may find, therefore, that a wine from the village of Puligny Montrachet in the Côte de Beaune has the commune name – Puligny Montrachet – as its sole AC; that it carries instead the AC of a grand cru vineyard, e.g. Chevalier Montrachet, within the village; or that it has a premier cru together with the commune as its AC, e.g. Puligny Montrachet Les Pucelles. Most ACs in the southern areas of Burgundy use district names, as in Bordeaux. General Burgundy areas are Bourgogne, Bourgogne Aligoté, Bourgogne Grand Ordinaire, Bourgogne Ordinaire and Bourgogne Passe Tout Grains. The grands crus and premiers crus referred to above have not been listed here.

CHABLIS
Chablis
Chablis premier cru
Petit Chablis

CÔTE DE NUITS (Côte d'Or)
Bourgogne Hautes Côtes de Nuit
Chambolle Musigny
Côte de Nuits Villages
Fixin
Gevrey Chambertin
Morey St Denis
Nuits St Georges
Vosne Romanée
Vougeot

CÔTE DE BEAUNE (Côte d'Or)
Aloxe Corton
Auxey Duresses
Beaune
Blagny
Bourgogne Hautes Côtes de Beaune
Chassagne Montrachet
Chorey les Beaune
Côte de Beaune
Côte de Beaune Villages
Dezizes les Maranges
Meursault
Monthélie
Pernand Vergelesses
Pommard
Puligny Montrachet

St Aubin
St Romain
Sampigny les Maranges
Santenay
Savigny
Volnay

CHALONNAISE
Givry
Mercurey
Montagny
Rully

MÂCONNAIS
Mâcon
Mâcon Supérieur
Mâcon Villages
Pinot Chardonnay Mâcon
Pouilly Fuissé

Pouilly Loché
Pouilly Vinzelles
St Véran

BEAUJOLAIS
Beaujolais
Beaujolais Supérieur
Brouilly
Chénas
Chiroubles
Côte de Brouilly
Fleurie
Juliénas
Morgon
Moulin à Vent
St Amour
There are also about 30 specified ACs for Beaujolais Villages.

CÔTES DU RHÔNE

Château Grillet
Châteauneuf-du-Pape
Chatillon en Diois
Clairette de Die
Condrieu

Cornas
Coteaux de Triscastin
Côtes du Rhône
Côtes du Rhône Villages
Côte Rôtie

Côte du Ventoux
Crozes Hermitage
Gigondas
Hermitage
Lirac

St Joseph
St Péray
Tavel

LOIRE

Anjou
Anjou Coteaux de la Loire
Bonnezeaux
Cabernet d'Anjou
Cabernet de Saumur
Coteaux de l'Aubance
Coteaux du Layon
Coteaux du Layon Chaume
Quarts de Chaume

Rosé d'Anjou
Saumur
Saumur Champigny
Savennières

Muscadet
Muscadet des Coteaux de la Loire
Muscadet de Sèvre et Maine

Pouilly sur Loire
Pouilly Fumé

Quincy

Reuilly

Sancerre
Menetou Salon

Touraine
Bourgueil
Chinon
Montlouis
St Nicholas de Bourgueil
Touraine Amboise
Touraine Azay le Rideau
Touraine Mesland
Vouvray

ALSACE
In Alsace the specific ACs take their designations from the grape variety, not the region. General ACs are Alsace and Alsace grand cru.

Gewürztraminer
Muscat d'Alsace

Pinot Blanc
Pinot Noir

Riesling
Silvaner

Tokay d'Alsace

allowed, their acreage, yield and the way in which the wine has been made are all subject to control and although once again there is no guarantee that you will like the wine, it is recognized to be of superior quality. In any vintage the amount of wine allowed to receive the AC accolade is strictly limited. In theory, a grower could make as much 'AC' wine as he liked, but he will only be allowed to apply the designation to a predetermined maximum number of bottles. The object of this regulation is to encourage the grower to make better wine rather than more wine. Only 17 per cent of French wine production receives the AC label. In Burgundy full AC is frequently conferred on single vineyards; in Bordeaux they extend to communes as well.

Champagne is so distinguished a wine that although it possesses an appellation contrôlée, it does not have to exhibit an AC authority: the description 'Champagne' or 'Vin de Champagne' is more than adequate. Its production is scrupulously controlled and the word alone carries an enviable guarantee of

OPPOSITE *A large percentage of exported French wine carries the AC designation. This is a brief guide to some of the AC names, by region.*

authenticity. As with all wines, if a year is named on the bottle it means that the bottle contains only the wine of the named year. A non-vintage wine is a blend of years.

There are also special classifications for the wine-growing areas of Bordeaux, Burgundy and Champagne given to vineyards of outstanding quality.

WORDS TO NOTE

BORDEAUX WINES:
Mis (mise) en bouteilles au château means that the wine has been bottled by the estate which has produced the wine. The château is simply the property: it can be anything from a small farmhouse to a grand turreted castle and it includes the whole vineyard. Thus Château Palmer denotes the vineyards and the estate where those particular wines are produced. By and large the word château is confined to the estates of Bordeaux.
Grand Vin is a phrase with no legal significance which means 'great wine'.
Cru Classé denotes an estate classified according to a degree of excellence first laid down in 1855 but subsequently revised and extended. The *crus* (which simply means 'growths') which you will

see alluded to are in descending order of excellence: Premier, Deuxième, Troisième, Quatrième, Cinquième, Exceptionnel, Bourgeois Supérieur, Bourgeois.

BURGUNDY WINES:
Domaine is the Burgundian equivalent of château, thus *Mise en bouteilles au Domaine* means bottled at the property. *Mise en bouteilles par la propriétaire* indicates that it was bottled by the grower but not necessarily at the domaine. Sometimes this takes place in the region, sometimes miles away.
Récolte: vintage.
Grand Cru, first class vineyard; *Premier Cru*, second class vineyard. Unlike Bordeaux, Burgundy wines were not classified in 1855; as a result, there are today far fewer classifications in the region.
Négociant, a man who buys wine, ages it, bottles it and ships it. He plays an important role in creating good wines and in Burgundy there are many négociants of impeccable reputation (and some peccable ones too).

CHAMPAGNES:
Blanc de Blancs: made solely from white grapes. The degrees of sweetness are: *Brut*, completely dry; *Extra Sec*, dry; *Sec*, sweetish; *Demi-Sec*, sweet; *Doux*, very sweet.

OTHER WORDS TO NOTE

vigneron, wine grower; *pétillant*, slightly sparkling; *côte*, a slope on which vines grow; *clos*, an enclosed vineyard; *chai*, wine store or warehouse.

A leisurely glass of wine in the afternoon sunshine – one of the many pleasures of France.

Germany

The wines of Germany are more strictly regimented and delimited than any others in the world. With their obsessive interest in minutiae the Germans have devised a system whereby a bottle of quality wine bought in a restaurant can be traced back to the very cask from which it came. The new German wine laws take into account the climatic variations which exist in what is the most northerly wine-growing region of the world. It is important to know the name of the vineyard because its micro-climate may be entirely different from a vineyard 200 yards away; indeed the variety and individuality of German wines is unparalleled elsewhere.

The German language is highly polysyllabic and at first sight looks like some terrifying gobbledegook. I have a label in front of me for one of the great German wines of the century. It reads: *1959 Canzemer Alternburg Trockenbeerenauslese Bischoeffisches Priesterseminar.* That tells you that the wine is a 1959 vintage from Canzem in the Saar made from grapes left to dry on the vine and gathered almost one by one in the vineyard of Altenburg owned by the Theological Seminary!

The new German Federal Law has defined 11 regions, 31 districts, 130 general sites and 2,600 individual sites where wine is made under strict controls. The classic German wine bottle is tall and tapering; the Rhine wines are bottled in brown glass, the Mosel wines in green. The wines of Franken (Franconia) come in a flagon or flask-shaped bottle called a *bocksbeutel*.

On the label you will see, where appropriate, the year of the vintage, the region where the wine was produced, the parish, the specific vineyards, the grape, the name of the producer or shipper, the AP (*Amtliche Prüfungsnummer*; its certificate of authenticity); the type and category of wine and where it was bottled. An identification number further authenticates the wine's provenance.

The qualities of wine begin humbly with *Tafelwein* – table wine which may be a blend of German and other EEC wines. *Deutscher Tafelwein* is made from grapes produced in five authorized regions: Main, Rhine, Mosel, Neckar and Oberrhein.

Qualitätswein bestimmter Anbaugebiete (QbA) is a quality wine from a specific region. The best-known wine in this category is Liebfraumilch.

Qualitätswein mit Prädikat is quality wine with a special attribute. The degrees are:

A *Kabinett*, an above-average wine usually made from the produce of a single vineyard.

B *Spätlese*, wine made from late-gathered, ripe grapes.

C *Auslese*, wine made from selected fully mature grape bunches.

D *Beerenauslese*, wine made only from the ripest of the grapes in those bunches.

E *Trockenbeerenauslese*, wine made from grapes which have been shrivelled by noble rot.

F *Eiswein*, wine from grapes allowed to freeze on the vine. The rarest Eiswein made for over two centuries was picked on the morning of 12 January 1980 when the temperature in Bingen was −10°C. As it grew light a small group of pickers made their frozen way into the vineyard of Scharlachberg to collect the last grapes of the 1979 vintage. The grapes, like small berries, were frozen as hard as stones and the concentration of sugar was immense. So rich in sugar is the wine that it will certainly not reach its peak of perfection for perhaps 50 years or more. Its rarity (only 1,780 bottles have been made) could make the eventual sale price the highest ever recorded for a German wine.

WORDS TO NOTE:

Bereich, one of the 31 districts producing quality wine; *Diabetiker Weinsiegel*, wine seal given to wines with no more than four grammes per litre of residual sugar; *Einzellage*, vineyard; *Erzeugerabfüllung*; wine bottled by grower; *Oechsle*, a measure of the alcoholic strength of the grape must.

The Mosel and Rhine regions of Germany produce wines strikingly different in character. Shown here, Zell on the river Mosel (left) and a Nierstein riesling vineyard on the Rhine (right).

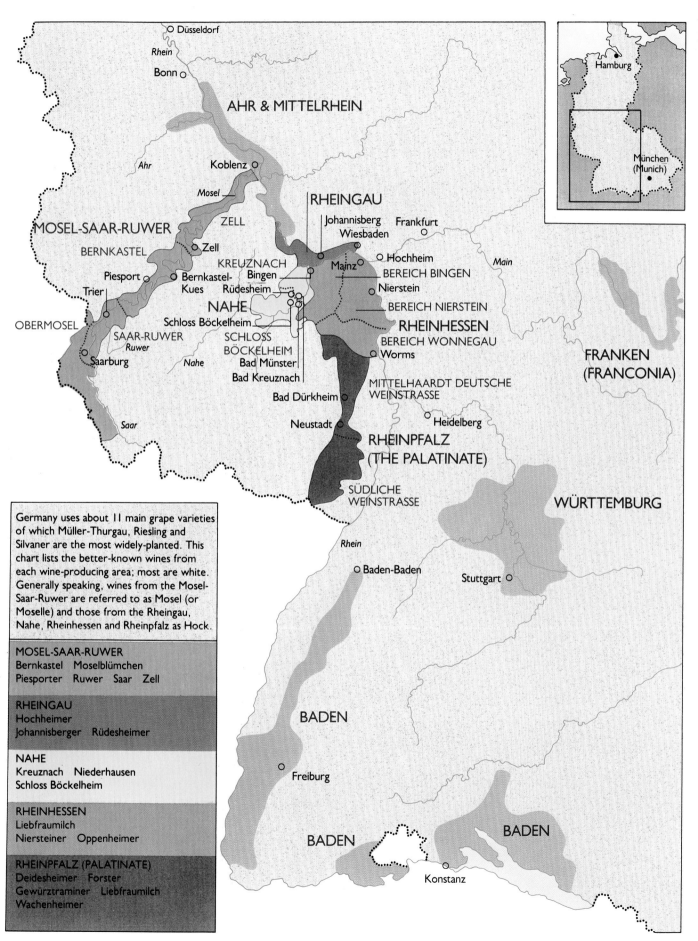

AHR & MITTELRHEIN

MOSEL-SAAR-RUWER

BERNKASTEL

OBERMOSEL

SAAR-RUWER

ZELL

RHEINGAU

KREUZNACH

NAHE

SCHLOSS BÖCKELHEIM

BEREICH BINGEN

BEREICH NIERSTEIN

RHEINHESSEN

BEREICH WONNEGAU

MITTELHAARDT DEUTSCHE WEINSTRASSE

RHEINPFALZ (THE PALATINATE)

SÜDLICHE WEINSTRASSE

FRANKEN (FRANCONIA)

WÜRTTEMBURG

BADEN

BADEN

BADEN

Düsseldorf

Bonn

Koblenz

Ahr

Mosel

Rhein

Zell

Piesport

Trier

Saarburg

Ruwer

Saar

Nahe

Bernkastel-Kues

Bingen

Rüdesheim

Bad Münster

Bad Kreuznach

Schloss Böckelheim

Johannisberg

Wiesbaden

Mainz

Hochheim

Nierstein

Worms

Bad Dürkheim

Neustadt

Heidelberg

Frankfurt

Main

Rhein

Baden-Baden

Stuttgart

Freiburg

Konstanz

Hamburg

München (Munich)

Germany uses about 11 main grape varieties of which Müller-Thurgau, Riesling and Silvaner are the most widely-planted. This chart lists the better-known wines from each wine-producing area; most are white. Generally speaking, wines from the Mosel-Saar-Ruwer are referred to as Mosel (or Moselle) and those from the Rheingau, Nahe, Rheinhessen and Rheinpfalz as Hock.

MOSEL-SAAR-RUWER
Bernkastel   Moselblümchen
Piesporter   Ruwer   Saar   Zell

RHEINGAU
Hochheimer
Johannisberger   Rüdesheimer

NAHE
Kreuznach   Niederhausen
Schloss Böckelheim

RHEINHESSEN
Liebfraumilch
Niersteiner   Oppenheimer

RHEINPFALZ (PALATINATE)
Deidesheimer   Forster
Gewürztraminer   Liebfraumilch
Wachenheimer

Italy

In 1963 the Italian government established rules for the national control of the wine industry, the world's largest, with some 9,000,000 acres of vines under cultivation. At least 100 grape varieties are planted and there are several hundred different types of wine, so regulating what was very much a fragmented industry did not prove easy. Much of the wine is produced by small growers owning less than a hectare each – a hectare is 2.4 acres.

The *Denominazione di Origine Controllata* were based on the French model and there are three categories:

A *Denominazione Semplice*, a statement of the region where the wine is produced.

B *DOC*, a controlled wine. Since 1963 almost 200 wines have achieved this category.

C *DOCG*, a wine controlled and guaranteed (*garantita*); this certificate is only awarded to the finest wines.

A national committee on which representatives of both government and industry sit assesses applications for DOC and DOCG and makes recommendations to the appropriate Ministry for the award of the Presidential Decree.

On the label the name of the area, district or commune may appear or the wine may be described by its grape. The word *classico* as in Chianti Classico indicates that the wine has come from the best yielding part of the Chianti area. The rules are enforced at local level by the *consorzi* or consortium of growers and a neck label often denotes superior quality.

Although many Italian wines and in particular those of Chianti are bottled in straw-covered flasks, there is a move towards bottling the finer wines in conventional Bordeaux-shaped bottles.

WORDS TO NOTE

Frizzante, semi-sparkling; *spumante*, sparkling; *vecchio*, old; *bianco*, white; *rosso*, red; *rosato*, rosé; *secco*, dry; *amabile*, medium sweet; *dolce*, sweet; *abboccato*, slightly sweet; *amaro*, bitter; *casa vinicola*, wine house; *fiasco*, flask; *imbottigliato*, bottled; *riserva*, wine matured for a specified number of years; *superiore*, wine made from selected grapes with comparative age and high alcoholic strength; *vendemmia*, vintage; *vino da tavola*, ordinary honest everyday wine.

Young grape vines in the Martina Franca district of Puglia in Italy. The conical roofs in the background are characteristic of the region.

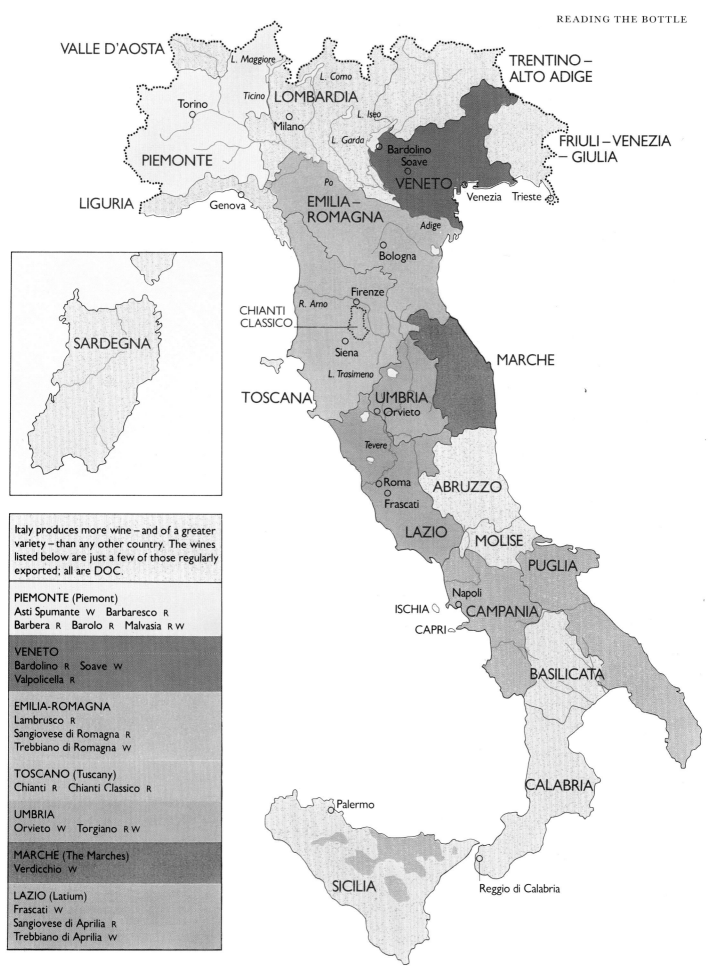

VALLE D'AOSTA

L. Maggiore

TRENTINO –
ALTO ADIGE

L. Como

LOMBARDIA

Ticino

Torino

L. Iseo

Milano

FRIULI – VENEZIA
– GIULIA

PIEMONTE

L. Garda

Bardolino
Soave

VENETO

Po

EMILIA –
ROMAGNA

Venezia   Trieste

LIGURIA

Genova

Adige

Bologna

SARDEGNA

Firenze

R. Arno

CHIANTI
CLASSICO

MARCHE

Siena

L. Trasimeno

TOSCANA

UMBRIA

Orvieto

Tevere

Roma
Frascati

ABRUZZO

LAZIO

MOLISE

PUGLIA

Napoli

ISCHIA

CAMPANIA

CAPRI

BASILICATA

CALABRIA

Palermo

SICILIA

Reggio di Calabria

Italy produces more wine – and of a greater variety – than any other country. The wines listed below are just a few of those regularly exported; all are DOC.

PIEMONTE (Piemont)
Asti Spumante W   Barbaresco R
Barbera R   Barolo R   Malvasia R W

VENETO
Bardolino R   Soave W
Valpolicella R

EMILIA-ROMAGNA
Lambrusco R
Sangiovese di Romagna R
Trebbiano di Romagna W

TOSCANO (Tuscany)
Chianti R   Chianti Classico R

UMBRIA
Orvieto W   Torgiano R W

MARCHE (The Marches)
Verdicchio W

LAZIO (Latium)
Frascati W
Sangiovese di Aprilia R
Trebbiano di Aprilia W

61

Spain, famous for its sherry, and Portugal, equally famous for its port, both now export increasing amounts of unfortified wines. Rioja produces the best-known Spanish still wines, but those from other areas are gaining in popularity. Pink table wine is the principal export from Portugal.

RIOJA
Rioja Tinto R (full-bodied)
Rioja Clarete R (lighter)
Rioja Blanco W

PENEDES
Sparkling whites; still wines R W P

TARRAGONA
Sweet fortified wines

PRIORATO
Dry reds

LA MANCHA
Valdepeñas

JEREZ
Sherry

MÁLAGA
Málaga (dark, sweet wine)

MONTILLA
Montilla

MINHO
Vinho Verde R W

DOURO
Port

DÃO
Non-fortified reds; a few whites

MADEIRA
Madeira

BELOW *Working a vineyard in the Rioja region of Spain.*

62

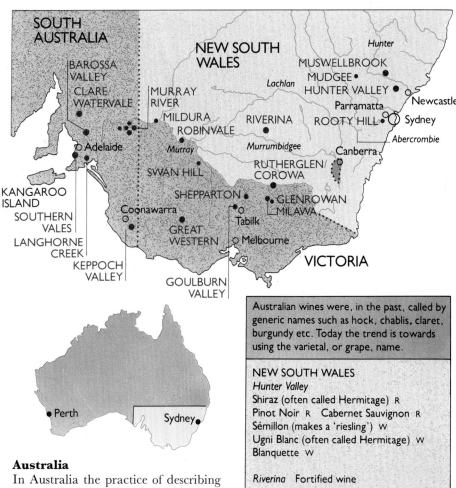

Spain

If Germany suffers from an excess of wine bureaucracy, Spain is just the reverse. Although it has a greater acreage under grapes than Italy, Spain produces only half as much wine; much of the production comes from small and unsupervised vineyards. although wine intended for export is subject to laboratory analysis. The best wines carry a *Denominación de Origen*. The most organized part of the Spanish wine industry is centred round the sherry-making area of Jerez.

WORDS TO NOTE

Clarete, light red wines with a strong bouquet; *blanco*, white; *tinto*, red; *rosado*, pink; *seco*, dry; *dulce* or *abocado*, sweet; *espumoso*, sparkling; *reservas*, wines aged for a number of years in wood.

BELOW *The Douro Valley in Portugal, where the grapes for port are grown, gathered, fermented and blended with spirit before being shipped to Oporto.*

Australia

In Australia the practice of describing wines by their generic European names (Burgundy, Claret, Sauternes) has been largely discontinued. Imperial preference once encouraged the export of large quantities of strong and rather horrid sweet red wine known in Britain as Empire Burgundy. Now that the Empire has gone Australia has created a new image for itself and its finer wines are of excellent quality and value.

The labels tend to be richly endowed with information and reading them can last you well into the coffee stage of a meal. I wouldn't be surprised to find one day the name of the person who operated the corking machine included on the label. At the Hungerford Hill vineyard they almost clock up the hour of fermenting. 'The Sémillon grapes', reads one of their labels, 'were vintaged under controlled fermentation and bottled on June 9, 1971. Picking date February 8, 1971. Gallons vintaged 3500.'

Another vineyard, Metala, obviously not bothered with industrial espionage, prints on the label: 'After three years maturing in 500-gallon oak casks it was filled into 30,672 pint bottles and this is

Australian wines were, in the past, called by generic names such as hock, chablis, claret, burgundy etc. Today the trend is towards using the varietal, or grape, name.

NEW SOUTH WALES
Hunter Valley
Shiraz (often called Hermitage) R
Pinot Noir R   Cabernet Sauvignon R
Sémillon (makes a 'riesling') W
Ugni Blanc (often called Hermitage) W
Blanquette W

Riverina   Fortified wine

VICTORIA
Great Western   Sparkling wine

Goulburn Valley   Shiraz R

Coonawarra   'Claret' R

SOUTH AUSTRALIA
Barossa Valley & Southern Vales
Rhine Riesling W
Cabernet (often blended with Shiraz) R

bottle 14,921.' I must say I don't object to all this and indeed it does give you a pretty clear indication of what is inside the bottle. Houghton's 1970 Burgundy read: 'A full-bodied dry white wine which is only produced in Western Australia and developed as a distinctive White Burgundy style from Sémillon and Tokay grapes. The Indian Ocean plays an important part in the production of this wine. The long dry summer and cool oceans' breezes at night combine to eliminate the acidity found in grapes grown in colder climates. This wine leaves a pleasing softness on the palate and is usually served chilled.' Good on you, Blue!

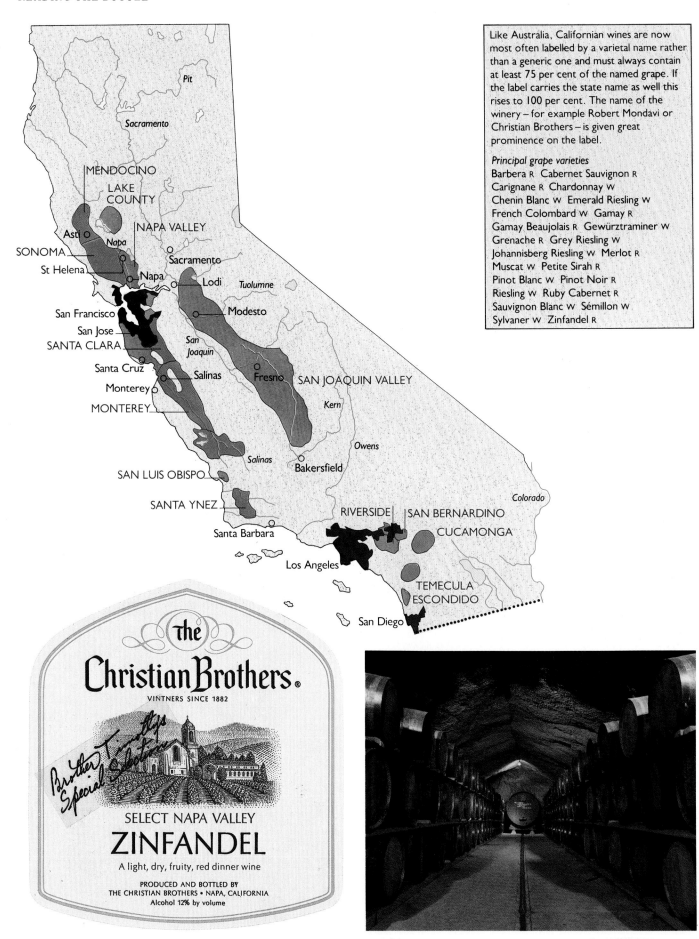

Pit

Sacramento

MENDOCINO
LAKE
COUNTY

NAPA VALLEY

Asti ○
Napa
SONOMA
St Helena
Napa
Sacramento
Lodi
Tuolumne
San Francisco
Modesto
San Jose
SANTA CLARA
San
Joaquin
Santa Cruz
Salinas
Fresno
SAN JOAQUIN VALLEY
Monterey ○
MONTEREY
Kern

Salinas
Owens
SAN LUIS OBISPO
Bakersfield

Colorado
SANTA YNEZ
RIVERSIDE   SAN BERNARDINO
CUCAMONGA
Santa Barbara

Los Angeles
TEMECULA
ESCONDIDO
San Diego

Like Australia, Californian wines are now most often labelled by a varietal name rather than a generic one and must always contain at least 75 per cent of the named grape. If the label carries the state name as well this rises to 100 per cent. The name of the winery – for example Robert Mondavi or Christian Brothers – is given great prominence on the label.

Principal grape varieties
Barbera R Cabernet Sauvignon R
Carignane R Chardonnay W
Chenin Blanc W Emerald Riesling W
French Colombard W Gamay R
Gamay Beaujolais R Gewürztraminer W
Grenache R Grey Riesling W
Johannisberg Riesling W Merlot R
Muscat W Petite Sirah R
Pinot Blanc W Pinot Noir R
Riesling W Ruby Cabernet R
Sauvignon Blanc W Sémillon W
Sylvaner W Zinfandel R

the
ChristianBrothers®
VINTNERS SINCE 1882

Brother Timothy's Special Selection

SELECT NAPA VALLEY
ZINFANDEL
A light, dry, fruity, red dinner wine

PRODUCED AND BOTTLED BY
THE CHRISTIAN BROTHERS • NAPA, CALIFORNIA
Alcohol 12% by volume

United States

As in Australia and South Africa the move is away from generic descriptions of wine to varietal identification. There are few detailed regulations governing the production of wine and much more emphasis is placed on the good name of the individual vineyard. It is still permitted by law to describe wine by the following names: Burgundy, Claret, Chablis, Champagne, Chianti, Hock, Malaga, Madeira, Moselle, Port, Rhine wine, Sauternes, Sherry and Tokay but the State of origin must be declared.

If a grape is named on the label Federal Law requires that 75 per cent of the grape must come from the region specified. State Laws vary but compared with France or Germany wine law is as yet in its infancy.

Although wine is produced in New York (10% of production); Illinois (2%); Virginia (0.6%); South Carolina and Michigan (0.4% each); Georgia (0.3%); Washington, New Jersey, Arkansas and Ohio (0.2% each) and Missouri (0.1%), it is California with 86 per cent of total production which dominates the industry.

Prominent on every Californian label is the name of the winery. Then comes the wine type and its legal classification. 'Table wine' must have an alcoholic content of less than 14 per cent, 'dessert wine' must contain between 17 and 24 per cent alcohol and 'sparkling wine' indicates that the wine has been fermented by the *cuve close* method. The description 'Champagne' is only allowed if the fermentation occurred in the bottle. If not it may only be described as 'champagne style' or 'champagne type'.

OPPOSITE *Wine resting in barrels in a Napa Valley cellar.*

South Africa's Cape Province has 15 demarcated areas for the production of 'Wines of Origin'. Certification seals with three bands of colour are placed around the necks of bottles from approved districts; blue gives the area of origin, red the vintage and green the grape variety used.

Principal grape varieties
Cabernet Sauvignon R
Cinsaut (Hermitage) R
Clairette Blanche W
Colombard W
Palomino W   Pinotage R
Riesling W   Shiraz R
Steen W (variety of Chenin Blanc)
Tinto Barocca R

Principal output of districts
LIGHT RED WINES
Constantia & Durbanville
Piketberg   Robertson
Stellenbosch   Worcester

FULL-BODIED RED WINES
Malmesbury   Stellenbosch

LIGHT AND DRY WHITE WINES
Coastal Region
Constantia & Durbanville   Piketberg
Stellenbosch   Tulbagh

MEDIUM TO SWEET WHITE WINES
Caledon   Montagu
Robertson   Stellenbosch
Swellendam   Worcester

DESSERT WINES
Boberg   Klein Karoo
Olifantsrivier

SOUTH AFRICAN SHERRY
Coastal Region
Olifantsrivier   Paarl
Stellenbosch   Tulbagh

South Africa

South Africa's Wine and Spirit Board has since 1972 strictly controlled the labelling and bottling of wine. Fifteen areas have been designated for the production of Wines of Origin and a number of outstanding individual estates have been nominated. An approved wine carries a blue, green and red seal round the neck which indicates the Board's accolade and reveals the area of origin, the year of vintage and the grape variety. As in Germany an identification number on the label serves to authenticate the wine which, through this number, can be traced back, if necessary, to the vineyard which made it.

'Estate' indicates that the wine originates in a demarcated area and even the term 'superior' can only be used for a wine which conforms in that respect to the Board's exacting standards.

65

Wine without Food

In New York and other American urban centres the cocktail hour has long been a ritual period of unwinding after the day's toil at telephone and Dictaphone. The theory seemed to be that you should anaesthetize your palate with four or five extra-dry jumbo martinis before moving to the table. Recently jogging has taken over and many cholesterol-conscious Americans will nowadays only permit a glass of dry white wine when the 'happy hour' strikes. In Britain, too, those who set trends are serving table wine as well as fortified wine before a meal. And that makes good sense. The role of the apéritif is not to deaden the palate and tastebuds but to awaken in them an anticipation for food.

As a general rule pre-meal drinks should be either cooled or chilled. Imagine having spent all day on the beach; a cold shower is more refreshing than a hot bath. So a cool glass of wine, a chilled sherry or a vermouth with ice are the drinks which stimulate and relax your guests in preparation for the table.

As host or hostess you should be relaxed as well. The most unrelaxing prelude to a meal is to be dashing around with three different kinds of spirit and five mixers and wondering whether that empty glass contains rum and coke, gin and tonic, vodka and vermouth or whisky and water. Serve only one drink and your problems are solved. If you make that one drink wine there is no reason why guests shouldn't carry their glasses to the table and finish their wine with the first course. So when choosing a wine try and match it to your starter. More of that in a moment; let's look first at some of the more conventional wine-based apéritifs.

Sherry is more universally acceptable than any other drink. Like all white wines it should be served cold, so an hour or so in the fridge before drinking is advisable, particularly for medium and dry blends. Although the finest sherries come only from the region around Jerez you must make up your own mind about the quality and style of sherry you wish to serve.

Manzanilla Very pale and dry with a faintly bitter almost salty tang. Some say it comes from the sea breezes which blow off the Atlantic over the vineyards and the bodegas of Sanlúcar de Barrameda at the mouth of the river Guadalquivir. Manzanilla is derived from the Spanish word *manzana* meaning crab–apple but its taste, although crisp, is not a bit like an apple.

OPPOSITE *A white wine punch, the perfect drink for a summer party.*
BELOW *The colour of sherry can be a consistent guide to its sweetness, though there are exceptions, such as the straw-coloured cream sherry. From left to right, those shown here range from the very sweet to the very dry.*

Fino Light and delicate, this is the greatest of all the sherries. Its unique bouquet comes from the *flor* or yeast which although imitated in other countries has never been perfectly reproduced. Pale gold in colour, this is to my mind the perfect apéritif; its delicacy is enhanced by chilling.

Amontillado The best amontillados are perfected by setting aside outstanding finos and allowing them to age in wood. Amontillado, a rich amber colour with a nutty bouquet, can be either medium-dry or medium-sweet. It has

more body than fino and is stronger in alcohol.

Oloroso The colour of dark gold, soft, mellow and usually encountered in its sweetened form. It is preferred, in Spain, in its natural dry state.

Brown sherry Made by blending olorosos with sweetening and colouring wines.

Cream sherries Sweet, rich, dark, smooth and as far as I'm concerned not suitable for drinking before a meal, although they are often ideal at the end of one. Bristol Milk is a brand that dates

Wine-based apéritifs, each with a distinctive taste. Pink vermouth is a relative newcomer to the wide range available.

back to the seventeenth-century and was a favourite of Samuel Pepys. According to Harveys, the famous Bristol shippers, towards the end of the last century an aristocratic French lady was visiting their cellars. Having tried the famous Bristol Milk she was then invited to taste an even finer though lesser-known blend. 'If that', she exclaimed, 'was milk, this must be cream.'

The cover to the sheet music of 'Champagne Charlie'. A companion comic song was 'Cool Burgundy Ben'.

Thus was Bristol Cream born.

If your own taste is for the very driest of sherries remember that for many people an amontillado is as 'dry' a sherry as they would ever wish to drink. It is therefore a good idea to have two kinds of sherry to offer, a medium and a dry. If you are tempted to serve a sherry sweeter than an amontillado remember that sweet wine before a meal tends to muffle the palate, not sharpen it; just as you wouldn't take a slice of cake before a prawn cocktail so an oloroso or cream sherry is not always the best of apéritifs.

Neither is **port**, although even here there is a singular exception. There is a white apéritif port which is extremely popular in Portugal and when served well chilled it may astonish you by its interesting balance between the full-bodied and the dry.

White vermouth served with ice and lemon is an excellent apéritif. An added advantage is that it can be diluted to the most innocuous strength with soda water or mixed (white with red or pink) to vary the degree of sweetness. Originally Italian vermouth was considered to be sweet and French dry, but these distinctions no longer apply.

There are many other wine and spirit–based apéritifs on the market: Dubonnet, Cap Corse, Lillet, Byrrh, Campari, Punt e Mes, Amer Picon, St Raphael, Fernet Branca, Selestat, Arquebuse, Suze, Bonal, Nicolet and Ambassadeur. They all have their aficionados and many of them, particularly when taken on the rocks, make an ideal summer drink. Not all these branded apéritifs are to everyone's taste and you may find a lack of enthusiasm for the more highly-flavoured.

So let's move on to wine and first of all **sparkling wine,** because it is as an apéritif that Champagne and most of the sparkling wines come into their own. Ideal for receptions, a glass of something bubbly looks good, and quickly lifts the spirit both psychologically and physiologically. The reason why carbonated wines are so perfect before a meal is that the CO_2 bubbles take the alcohol into the bloodstream far more quickly and the bubbles release their infinitesimal kick in your mouth rather than your stomach; you get an immediate lift at the portals of the body rather than in the crypt.

I have never yet been offered a glass of **Champagne** without feeling that I have been singled out for special attention. I might also add that I have never been offered Champagne with stout (Black Velvet) or Champagne with orange juice (Buck's Fizz) without feeling that two very good drinks have been ruined by being yoked so inharmoniously together. Stout and orange juice are excellent on their own and so is Champagne: that's the way it should remain. Champagne cocktails are another pre-dinner recipe for disaster. Mixing Champagne with brandy is a wasteful folly.

When costing a wedding reception, caterers will customarily suggest that you allow half a bottle of Champagne per guest, but with its quick-acting impact and its fairly high level of alcohol Champagne can be quite an economical drink when poured judiciously. The same is true of sparkling wines which are not entitled to the name Champagne. Austria, Cyprus, Hungary, Israel,

69

America, South Africa and Australia all produce sparkling wines (white, red and pink) but it is France which once again commands the market with its first-class sparkling wines from the Loire and Burgundy; Italy is noted for its 'spumante' wines; some outstanding sparkling wines both dry and sweet are produced in Spain while the sparkling German hocks and moselles and the 'sekt' made mainly from imported still wines are well worth trying.

If you decide to serve a **still wine** as an apéritif it is wisest to choose white. There are one or two exceptions. When the new Beaujolais arrives on the market in November it can make an interesting pre-dinner drink. Served chilled, its young fruity flavour, particularly if it is a good vintage, can be light and attractive but it cannot always be successfully followed by a white wine at the table. Recently the Italian house of Antinori introduced a 'vino novello' made to be drunk in the year of the vintage and a young Muscadet (*primeur*) is also obtainable.

What you really need in a wine to be drunk on its own before a meal is a freshness, a crispness perhaps; a wine without too much body, something young and easy to appreciate. There is such a wide choice here that it's difficult to know where to start. Wines which immediately spring to mind are those from the Loire, Alsace, the Rhine and the Moselle, the *vinhos verdes* (literally green or young wines) from Portugal, and wines like Soave and Frascati from Italy, all of which are pleasant and not too assertive. After all, the wine is to serve as an overture to a meal and does not have to compete with heavily orchestrated dishes.

Perhaps the ideal compromise wine is pink, or to give it its French name, *vin rosé*. It is, I think, a difficult wine – often too substantial for fish and too slight for meat. But drunk out-of-doors on a summer evening it is perfect, and it could be served equally well before a winter meal.

OPPOSITE *Wining before dining. From left to right: a young white* vinho verde *from Portugal, a Cape Riesling, a flowery raisiny* vin doux naturel *made from Muscat grapes in Beaumes-de-Venise, a white wine from the Verona area made from the Garganega di Soave grape, a dry Champagne, a medium-dry Italian sparkling pink wine and a light, medium-dry pink wine from Anjou in the Loire valley.*

The best French rosé, said to have been a favourite of François I, comes from Tavel near the mouth of the Rhône; an almost equally good rosé is made in nearby Lirac. Then there is the famous village of Marsannay on the Côte de Dijon in Burgundy whose rosé wines are made from the Pinot Noir grape. Equally prized are the rosé wines of the Loire and foremost among them are the Cabernet d'Anjou and the Rosé d'Anjou.

In the Graves region of Bordeaux some fine rosé wines are produced and Portugal produces one semi-sparkling carbonated rosé which, it is claimed, can be drunk happily all through a meal. This is a matter of opinion.

Rosé wines can be dry but they are usually medium-dry; some border on the oversweet and may be too saccharine for pre-meal enjoyment. As with all wines it pays to buy a bottle beforehand and try it yourself. If *you* like it then it is unlikely that your closest relatives and friends will dislike it.

But to return from pink to white wines and those which can be enjoyed on their own. A properly made Muscadet, for instance, racked off the lees with a good balance of fruit might make a very pleasing solo glass although it would fulfil itself even better with a plate of seafood.

Moving along the Loire from the Muscadet-producing Pays Nantaise to Vouvray we find the slightly sweeter Chenin Blanc producing wines which are fruity and fresh whether they are still or sparkling. It is this same Chenin Blanc which makes one of the better South African wines. A white Burgundy would be very attractive drunk on its own – Meursault, Mâcon Villages, Chablis, Saint-Véran, Pouilly-Fuissé, Beaujolais Blanc and Pouilly-Vinzelles are all easily appreciated.

There are plenty of reliable white wines produced in Italy. Soave from Veneto in northern Italy and Frascati, named after the town of that name near Rome, are well known but there are plenty of more quaffable wines – many of them made from the Trebbiano grape. Austrian wines made from that relative of the Riesling, the Welschriesling, are also light and fruity for pre-prandial enjoyment and Yugoslav and Hungarian Rieslings are cheap and ubiquitous.

It is here that German wines are at their best and the Niersteiner and Hocks make ideal drinking even if we are more oriented towards Liebfraumilch which can vary from dryish to sweetish depending on whose hand has been at the blending tank. Liebfraumilch must be made from Riesling, Sylvaner, or Müller-Thurgau grapes and much of it comes from the Rheinhessen area.

Many people are attracted by the white wines of Alsace and, above all, the spicy Gewürztraminers in the long-necked Flûte d'Alsace. The Sylvaners, the dry and fruity Rosé d'Alsace, the Muscat and the Tokay are all drunk as apéritifs by the well-trained Alsatian.

Portugal produces some excellent dry wine and in particular the famous *vinhos verdes*. Bordered by the Atlantic on the west the vineyards are exposed to a damp climate with moderately hot summers so the wines have a refreshingly noticeable acidity. Low in sugar and high in malic acid, the secondary fermentation dissipates the acidity and engenders a prickly and slightly sparkling effect on the tongue. We really have no word for this semi-sparkling condition; the French refer to it as *pétillance*. The *vinhos verdes* are not high in alcohol but drunk young their freshness makes them an ideal appetizer or indeed something to be drunk right through a meal. Like the white wines of the Dão region the *vinhos verdes* are more lemony than green in colour.

White wine can be mixed with other ingredients to alter, indeed sometimes improve, its taste. The best known drink in France is Kir, named after the gastronome, freedom fighter and sometime Mayor of Dijon, Canon Félix Kir. Order a Kir in Burgundy and you will be given a glass of Aligoté with its acidity counter-balanced by one part in five of cassis, a syrup made from the blackcurrants which grow plentifully on the upper slopes of the Côte d'Or. The syrup is fortified with 14–20 per cent of alcohol and the best cassis is made in Dijon.

In Burgundy the Aligoté is sometimes replaced by young red Beaujolais to produce a *rince cochon*. When mixed with Champagne the cocktail is known as a Kir Royale; a slightly less royal Kir could be created with any dry sparkling wine. When making Kir the secret is to add just enough of the blackcurrant liqueur to flavour but not oversweeten the wine.

The French also lace their white wine

with Crème de Myrtilles made by mixing dried extract of bilberries with alcohol. The name 'Myr' has been registered in Britain by an enterprising wine merchant who recommends mixing Crème de Myrtilles (35 proof) with a dry white Saumur wine, but as with Kir any reasonably pleasant white wine will serve.

If you are going to make a chilled white wine cup, bear in mind that it can be diluted with soda water or lemonade or ice. You could mix Riesling with cider, a dry white wine with white vermouth, Chablis with sherry, Loire wine with Cointreau. One of the most fashionable drinks in Paris is the apéritif created by Michel Oliver for his restaurant in the Rue de Lille; at the Bistrot de Paris the house-drink is young Beaujolais flavoured with *eau-de-vie de framboises* – and the red Gamay wine

and the dry distillation of raspberries go excellently together. Why not try a combination to your own liking? Buy a miniature of *eau-de-vie de poires* and see how it lifts a glass of white table wine. Pear with white wine makes a good dessert so there is no reason why it shouldn't provide an interesting apéritif. Some friends of ours who like to serve a modest white wine before a meal have been known in summer to pour it over sliced pears or peaches and serve it from the bowl. When the wine has been drunk the fruit makes a delicious end to the meal.

There will of course be occasions when a preference for red wine is right and logical. I'm thinking of those cold winter days when the teeth might well rattle at the thought of a chilled rosé from Provence. In the age of central heating and air–conditioning the mull-

ing of wine may well seem an anachronism but at Christmastide mulled wine is both seasonable and sensible. It is also an economical way of using inexpensive wine – upholstered with spices and added spirit, even the thinnest of wines gains stature. Although mulled wine should be soup-hot it should never be boiled; that way you just evaporate the alcohol. And remember that if you don't want too many cracked glasses you should place a spoon in the glass before you pour in the steaming punch.

In England there have traditionally been three popular punches: Cardinal made with claret, Pope with Champagne and Bishop with port.

There are many combinations of wine and brandy or assorted liqueurs. One of the pleasures of compiling such a punch is that everyone can be his own chef; there are no rules. It is always wise, however, if you are going to experiment, to try the recipe on a small scale pre-party prototype to ensure that on the day you won't be left with a bowl of something horrid that nobody wants. Making a punch or a wine cup is not an occasion for finishing up all the dregs in the drinks cupboard. Doing it that way is halfway to hangover time and a quickfire formula for losing your friends.

OPPOSITE *White wine and Crème de Myrtilles (bilberry) or Cassis (blackcurrant) mixed four- or five-to-one make, respectively, Myr and Kir. Champagne or sparkling wine adds a royal touch. Serve well chilled.*

LEFT *The best mnemonic for a hot punch was given by Colonel Peter Hawker in his* Hints to Young Shooters: *'One sour, two sweet, four strong, eight weak'. To the juice of one lemon add double the quantity of sugar or honey, four times the quantity of brandy and eight times the quantity of wine. Cinnamon and cloves are other essentials, nutmeg the ideal topping. The greatest punch of all time was concocted by Edward Russell, Admiral of the Mediterranean fleet. At a party in November 1694 he caused an enormous fountain in his garden to be filled with 4 hogsheads of brandy, 250 gallons of Malaga, 20 gallons of lime juice, 2500 lemons, 1300 pounds of sugar, 5 pounds of grated nutmeg and 8 hogsheads of water. The party lasted a week. Punch derives its name from the Hindustani word 'panch', meaning five. The original five ingredients were strong liquor, sugar, lemon, spices and water.*

Wine with Food·1

'What', I was asked the other day, 'would you drink with duck?' There are several answers, all of which require more questions first. Would the bird be roasted or accompanied with a rich sauce? Would it be hot or cold? What wines would be available? If there was only a sweet wine going I think I'd prefer to drink water. The answer would also depend on where I was eating this duck. If I were in Bordeaux I'd drink claret. If I were in Beaune or Dijon I'd probably settle for Burgundy. In Australia I'd take it with a Shiraz, and so on.

The gastronomy of Europe has grown up alongside the vineyards. Wine in the pot, wine in the glass; it is a communion sanctified by centuries of usage. For a Frenchman or an Italian to sit down at the table without a glass of wine is unthinkable. A meal without wine, as has been aptly said, is like a day without sunshine.

It is always worth finding out what sort of food the people who live in wine-producing countries take with their wine. They've been matching wine with food unselfconsciously for centuries and if one or two good combinations haven't emerged then it

won't be for want of experiment. For comparison we'll see how the kitchen and the cellar combine in different countries to produce classically good meals.

France
When it comes to eating and drinking, France is not one country but many distinctive regions each with its own traditional specialities. None is greater than **Burgundy** which boasts that gastronomic marathon known as *Les Trois Glorieuses*, a series of meals held in the third weekend of November to coincide with the annual wine auctions at Beaune which attract members of the wine trade from all over the world. On the Saturday night the Confrérie des Chevaliers du Tastevin, the Burgundy wine order, holds a splendid banquet in the cellars of the sixteenth-century Clos de Vougeot, a vineyard originally founded by Cistercian monks. I attended one of these dinners and I recall sitting down to eat at eight and not rising until nearly one in the morning. The meal was unrushed and there was a great deal of singing by the Cadets de Bourgogne, joyous fanfares and much speech-making which spaced out so lavish a

succession of dishes matched with such perfect wines that the occasion is worth recalling.

The meal began with *Le Saladier de Jambon Persillé Dijonnaise relevé de bonne Moutarde Forte de Dijon*, a galantine made by simmering a whole ham with pig's trotters and white wine. The meat is then crushed and shredded, mixed with parsley and covered with jelly and served with France's most famous mustard made in Dijon with *verjus*, the acid juice of unripe grapes. With this was served a two-year-old Saint-Véran made from the white Chardonnay grape. The most famous wine of Mâcon is undoubtedly Pouilly–Fuissé. St Véran, which produces only 18,000 cases a year compared with the 550,000 cases of Pouilly–Fuissé, is a lesser wine which was only given its *appellation* in 1971; it is rapidly gaining popularity in Britain as a lesser-priced substitute for its more famous neighbour.

The ham was followed by turbot which was accompanied by another Chardonnay wine, a Meursault-Charmes with a full and nutty style, round in the mouth and again, drunk young at three years old, it was mellow and rich, perfect with turbot.

Then came a *Cassolettes de Cailles aux Morilles*, quail cooked with mushroom-like morels which give the bird a subtly earthy flavour. The wine with the quail was a Savigny-les-Beaunes, a soft fragrant Pinot Noir wine, light, fresh and early-maturing. After that a haunch of venison roasted and garnished with braised chestnuts and served with a gooseberry and pepper sauce. The Morey-St Denis we drank with it was a rich sturdy red wine big enough to stand up against the strong deer meat.

With the cheeses we drank a Latricières-Chambertin 1966, at that

OPPOSITE *Matching food and wine from the same country makes good sense. Shown here: pâté, goulash and cassata, with a Beaujolais-Villages, Bull's Blood and a slightly sweet (abboccato) Orvieto.*

LEFT *A market stall in Marseilles displays an abundance of unusual local seafoods.*

time eight years old. Chambertin is the greatest red wine of Burgundy and this example from a fine year was rightly kept to the end of the meal; a wine officially rated as a Grand Cru with the deep colour and finesse of the best wines of Burgundy.

Few of us eat meals of this quality more than once or twice in a lifetime, if at all. Its inclusion here is not simply to whet appetites; for when you consider the delicacy and complexity of the foods served, it is a perfect example of the way in which Burgundians are able to choose exactly the right native wines to complement their superlative cuisine.

Burgundy is famous for its Charollais cattle and *Boeuf à la bourguignonne*, beef cooked in red wine with onions, mushrooms and diced bacon. Its other internationally renowned wine dishes are *coq au vin*, young chicken stewed in wine, and its posher relative *coq au chambertin*. *Ecrevisses à la nage* are crayfish cooked in a white wine *court bouillon* and a *matelote à la bourguignonne* is a freshwater fish stew made with red Burgundy and Marc de Bourgogne. With so many wine-based dishes, it's important that the wines for drinking don't compete too much. What could be better than many of the wines of the region made from the Pinot Noir – elegant, with a delicate aroma and made to be drunk fairly young?

The vineyards of Burgundy stretch for over 200 kilometres and they are planted on south-facing sheltered slopes of which the most prized is the Côte d'Or. Within the Côte d'Or, Côte de Nuits runs from Dijon down to Nuits-St Georges and the Côte de Beaune surrounds the ancient town of Beaune. Further south are the vineyards of the Chalonnais, Mâconnais and Beaujolais. The Pinot Noir vine doesn't do very well on the granite soil of Beaujolais where the predominant grape is the Gamay. The classic white wine of the Côte de Beaune and the crisp wines of the Mâconnais come from the golden Chardonnay grape.

The **Côtes-du-Rhône** lies between Vienne and Avignon and the red wines are made from a mixture of up to 16 different permitted grapes. These are

OPPOSITE *The classic Burgundian dish, coq au vin – young chicken cooked in wine with lean breast of pork, onions, garlic, herbs and mushrooms. With it a red, soft, full-bodied burgundy of the Hautes Côtes de Beaune. Ideally the same wine should be in the pot.*

full purple-coloured wines the most famous of which are Hermitage and Châteauneuf-du-Pape. Being to the south of Burgundy the wines are more sun-baked and therefore more full-bodied.

The white wines of the region are full-bodied but generally dry and crisp; the pink wines, of which the most renowned is Tavel, are made principally from the Grenache. Provence to the south has had a noticeable influence on the cuisine of the Rhône and garlic and olive oil are to the fore.

Pâtés, wine stews, garlic soups, fish flavoured with fennel, lamb cooked with rosemary, snails cooked with white wine, artichokes, courgettes, aubergines, pomegranates, peaches and apricots, radishes and golden Chasselas table grapes cry out for Rhône wines ranging from the driest to the sweet Muscat de Beaumes de Venise.

Provençal cookery is even more spicy and highly flavoured. Garlic is enriched with herbs like thyme, savory, sage and basil and the huge Provençal tomato comes into its own in dishes like *poulet sauté aux tomates* or served on its own stuffed with meat or as *tomates à l'antiboise*, filled with a mixture of herbs, breadcrumbs, tuna and anchovies.

Mayonnaise with garlic, ratatouille, red mullet with rosemary, sea bass with fennel, sea-bream with tomatoes and garlic, sea-urchin soup, and anchovy, onion, tomato and olive tart are all eaten with the excellent red, rosé and white wines of Côtes de Provence, Bandol, Cassis and Bellet.

There is an equal cornucopia of food in **Roussillon** to the west where the white wines, sharp and relatively high in alcohol, are made by an early harvesting. These are excellent with fish, shellfish and the local stew, *zarzuela* (made from squid), mussels, hake or coalfish, lobster and lots of olive oil.

The VDQS pink wines harmonize well with hors d'oeuvre, sausage, poultry and meat flavoured with Catalan sauce. Roast pork prepared in the Catalonian way with garlic and orange can be drunk with white or pink wine.

The full-bodied red wines which draw their aromatic flavour from the Grenache grape and their backbone from the Carignan grape are excellent with game, grilled snails, grilled meat, black pudding, lamb chops, and cheese.

If in Burgundy those concerned with such things choose the wine to go with

the food then in **Bordeaux**, land of great bottles, a meal will often be planned round the wine. The oysters of Arcachon, the lampreys which are cooked *à la Bordelaise* in a rich dark wine sauce, the Pauillac lamb, the chicken and *foie gras* create a cuisine which is elegant and sophisticated.

Because the finest clarets do not welcome too much competition there is a great deal of beef eating and the meat is frequently grilled over a fire of vine branches (*grillé aux sarments*) or served as *entrecôte à la Bordelaise* in a wine, butter and shallot sauce or *entrecôte marchand de vin* with a red wine sauce.

In Bordeaux the diversity of soils produces a gratifying diversity of wines to make what is indisputably the most famous wine-growing region in the world. The Médoc is a large area producing mainly red wines which have tremendous finesse and take many years to mature. The wines of St Emilion tend to mature earlier than those of the Médoc but they have a fine colour and a mellow flavour and are stronger in alcohol. Their tannin content is lower than the wines of the Médoc due to the presence of the Merlot grape. Halfway between these two wines in character comes Pomerol, and then gravelly Graves which produces some excellent red wine but is mainly known for its fine white wines.

If the clarets are the greatest red wines in the world, the whites of the Sémillon grape reach their peak in the deep-coloured, golden, honeyed wines of Sauternes and Barsac, some of which can last for 100 years and more. The most famous of all the Sauternes is Château d'Yquem, so expensive that it is only drunk in Britain reverently by the glass. But in the Sauternes district you will find growers who claim that their unctuous, sweet wine can be enjoyed right through a meal.

The present Mayor of Sauternes, Comte Alexandre de Lur-Saluces, is the owner of Château Yquem which has been in his family since 1785. In 1855, alone among the wines of Bordeaux, the wine of Yquem was given the unique classification of a Premier Grand Cru. D'Yquem is so perfectly made a wine that it takes the yield of one vine to produce a single glass. The popular conceit that sophisticated palates call for dry wines is not shared by the owner of Yquem who, with every great vintage at his disposal from the mid-nineteenth

century onwards, told me a year or two ago that he thinks it goes well with all sorts of good food.

'We have it very commonly with *foie gras*, with *turbot sauce mousselin*, with all poultry and white meats, with Roquefort cheese. You can make a whole meal with d'Yquem.' Melon, salmon, trout, sole, oysters and mussels, calves' kidneys, game, fruits and sorbets have all been taken with Sauternes and

enjoyed by gourmets; proof, if proof at this stage were needed, that anything goes with anything as long as you think it does.

One finds the same proprietorial attitude to the product in **Champagne.** In Rheims you will be told that Champagne is the perfect accompaniment to every course and indeed if you go there as a guest of the trade you will drink little else. But it is a wine of some

Food and wine from Provence. The tomate à l'antiboise, *a big juicy tomato filled with a mixture of tuna fish, herbs and breadcrumbs latticed with anchovies and decorated with black olives, is surrounded by* crudités, *or sliced raw vegetables. Aïoli (garlic mayonnaise), that great Provençal favourite, is a perfect accompaniment to the* crudités. *The wine is a VDQS from the Côtes de Luberon in southeast France, which produces mainly white and pink wines.*

Vouvray, the most famous white wine of Touraine, is made from the Chenin Blanc grape. Depending on the year and the method of vinification Vouvray can appear in a variety of guises from the bone-dry to the rich and unctuous. A fruity, flowery gold-coloured wine with a suggestion of quince, a suitable Vouvray could be found to go with a pudding (as the lemon soufflé cased in flaked hazelnuts shown here), a soft cream cheese or a pâté.

acidity and, in my opinion, even at a quarter the price you would not necessarily plan a whole meal round this, the greatest sparkling wine in the world.

The dishes of Champagne show far less influence from the wine of the region than is the case in, say, Burgundy or Bordeaux. Bubbles, expensively induced, tend to disappear immediately they hit a saucepan or a frying pan, so cooking with Champagne can be a self-

defeating hobby. Champagne has, however, always featured largely in the cuisine of the great gastronomic houses. Carême, who was chef to the Emperor of Russia, used it by the crate when cooking and even today five-star restaurants prepare such foods as hare, partridge, venison, mutton, chicken, veal and trout in Champagne. Again, proof that in cooking and eating there are few combinations which someone is

79

not happy to experiment with and perfect.

Alsace also produces wines which are becoming increasingly popular exports. Although as in Champagne wine has not influenced the food deeply, Alsatians are happy to drink their white wines with dishes for which we might well choose a red. Thus they will open a bottle of the light, refreshing Sylvaner to go with sauerkraut and sausage, smoked shoulder of pork, truffled pig's trotter, snails, onion pie and pork pie.

The fuller-bodied Riesling with its fruity overtones and subtle bouquet would be chosen to accompany bacon tart, trout, fish stew, chicken, pheasant and cheesecake. The spicy Gewürztraminer is consumed more towards the end of a meal, with dishes like kirsch soufflé, apple tarts and quetsche plum pie.

Wherever you go in France you'll find the same comforting truth: the wines of the region go happily with the local food and there's very little fussing about what does or does not go with what. The fruity, light-bodied wines of Sancerre and Pouilly, with their distinctive bouquet, go perfectly with the small goat cheeses of Chavignol and the soft creamy cheeses like Chaource and Epoisse are delicious with a glass of chilled Chablis. In the Franche–Comté the local fondue is ideal accompanied by a well-chilled white wine of Arbois. The white wines of Savoie are matched with fish from Lac Léman; the grilled ortolan of the Landes is offered with the local Tursan red wine. A full-bodied Madiran from northwest of Pau is the natural wine for the local rabbit casserole with prunes; the wine of Cahors is a perfect partner for the famous cassoulet – beans, pig knuckles, preserved goose, pork rind and sausage; the wines of Languedoc–Roussillon, the Côtes–du–Rhône and Provence are all ideally matched with the fish and meat, the charcuterie, the stews and soups, the pastries and sweets which are prepared there in such mouth-watering abundance.

OPPOSITE *The traditional German Sauerbraten is marinated in wine and spices for 24–48 hours before cooking. Cucumbers, diced and mixed with sour cream and dill, help to offset the richness of the beef. Niersteiner is one of the better-known wines from the Rheinhessen, a district which also produces much Liebfraumilch. A Kabinett QmP, like this one, will generally be drier than other QmP wines.*

Germany

Nowhere in the world does the versatile Riesling grape grow more fruitfully and with such variety as it does around the winding rivers of the Rhine and Mosel. The Rieslings of the Mosel are fresh and dry; the Rhineland grapes yield full and fruity wine and elsewhere the wine is sweet and rich. This one vine produces a range of wine which can be drunk with every course from fish to fruit.

But the Germans tend to drink their quality wines, the Ausleses and above, on their own, before or after a meal; served, perhaps, with a few biscuits or a piece of cake.

In Germany white wines up to the sweetness of Auslese will be drunk with *pâté de foie gras*, fish, chicken or even lamb. The light fragrant red wines from the Ahr, Rheinhessen and Württemburg are frequently chosen to accompany baked fish, grilled dishes and game, beef, mutton, goose and duck. Sprightly Rieslings go well with cold and warm hor d'oeuvres, soups, egg dishes and shellfish. And fruity white wines with a full body are served with boiled or steamed white fish. The rich Traminer wines are taken with veal, pork and turkey and the popular cold meat and sausages are usually served with dry, strong wines from Franconia or the Palatinate.

German wine-makers strive to reach the perfection of a refreshing acidity balanced by the assertive fragrance of the grape. The wines of the Rheingau have this strong bouquet whereas the Nahe wines are lighter and crisper. The green-tinged Moselles with their Riesling bouquet often have a refreshing acidity and an occasional *spritzig* effervescence. The Franconian Steinweins are not dissimilar to the wines of Chablis but have much more fragrance. Unfortunately the invention by the Germans in the 1950s of a technique known as *Süssreserve*, in which unfermented grape juice is added to a dry wine high in acidity before bottling, has led to a large amount of oversweetening particularly among the cheaper German wines.

Hungary

Hungarian food is rich and filling and the wines of the country run the whole gamut of variety from the bone-dry white to the sweet and full. There are light pink wines and full-bodied red wines like Bull's Blood but the most famous of all is the luscious Tokay dessert wine. Discerning Hungarians might drink a light white Pécs Olasz Riesling with fish soup, a Bull's Blood with goulash soup, veal, lamb and chicken paprika. With English-type roasts, more Bull's Blood or the Szekszárd red wine. Sweetish or sweet wines like Móri Ezerjó, a muscatel, and heavy Tokay are recommended for the pudding and fruit stage.

Italy

Italy was named Enotria (wineland) by the Greeks, and it would take a large book to do justice to the wealth of wines produced there. From the northern Adige valley down to the sun-baked island of Sicily there is hardly a region without vines. Tuscan Chianti, the Asti Spumante, Barolo and Barbaresco of Piedmont, the white wines of Liguria, Soave, Valpolicella and Bardolino from Veneto; Lambrusco from Emilia–Romagna, Orvieto from Umbria – the output and variety is prodigious.

Italian food is of equal variety: soups, pasta, seafood, meat and fowl and an orchard of fruit. Because the Italians are historically a wine-drinking people they would take the subjects under discussion in these pages lightly; indeed they would not even be aware that there was any problem presented by the drinking of wine. Do we have a problem about the consumption of bread? White, brown, wholemeal, we'll take what's going. The Italians, unbothered by winelore or wineupmanship, drink the local wine, red, white, pink or sparkling, as it comes.

Barolo is a wine of fine deep colour, full-bodied and fruity. Made from the Nebbiolo grape it has been said to taste of tar and violets. Also made from the Nebbiolo grape is the full-bodied, rich, fragrant, deep in colour Barbaresco which at its best bears a DOCG label. Chianti is mellow in taste, perfumed and medium-bodied. Valpolicella, made round Lake Garda and Verona, is a light and lively wine, ruby red in colour. The famous white wine Soave is a clear pale-yellow dry wine at its best, sharp to the palate and ideal with fish.

For everyday eating try a Valpolicella or a Bardolino with antipasta, pâté or hors d'oeuvre, a Verdicchio with fish soup, Chianti or Barbera with spaghetti and meat or tomato sauce, salami or chili con carne. Steaks and stews are ideal with Barolo or

Chianti Classico and a Barbaresco goes well with kidneys.

I am a great admirer of the wines of Dr Giorgio Lungarotti, a pioneer wine-grower of Torgiano, which was one of the first districts to qualify for the DOC. The estate-bottled Lungarotti wines are internationally renowned. The dry white, pale gold in appearance, soft and delicate with a touch of fruitiness, is at its best served chilled with hors d'oeùvres, seafood, white meats, salads and cheese. The Rubesco has a deep ruby-red hue and is aged in oak casks and later in the bottle, a process which results in a round, fruity, well-balanced wine with good body and bouquet. Ideal with red meat, game, stews and cheese. The even more special *Riserva* is aged for at least three years in oak and equal to the biggest wines of Burgundy. Again a wine for rich red meat.

Pasta, the national dish of Italy, comes in all shapes and sizes and can be served with an endless variety of sauces. This tagliatelle, mixed after cooking with a sauce of tomatoes, peppers, mushrooms and ham, is shown with a DOC Chianti Classico – but would go equally well with any good dry or medium Italian wine. The dessert in the background is zabaglione, a frothy concoction made from the yolks of fresh eggs, sugar and white wine.

Spain is famous for its paella, a luscious mixture of shellfish and vegetables with a rice base. A good, light Rioja is a fine choice; if you shudder at the thought of red wine with fish, try a crisp, light white wine.

Spain

Spanish wine is now recovering from a sad period when most of its exports were cheap and not very pleasant; Spanish wine became synonymous with 'plonk'. Today that poor image is being replaced by a growing reputation for quality spearheaded by the fine table wines of Rioja where wines are selected, blended and aged with great skill, often being kept in cask for up to five years. The really outstanding Riojas have memorable depth of taste, and a slight vanilla-flavour acquired from their long ageing in wood.

The wines of Navarre, Valdeorras, Valdepeñas and Alella all blend well with the Spanish cuisine which is rich in garlic, tomatoes, olives and olive oil. White wines with gazpacho, paella and seafood; red with roast sucking pig, milk-fed lamb, chorizo and stews.

Wines from the rest of the world

Portugal

Famous most of all for its port, Portuguese table wines are now coming into their own and afford very good value. Half the wine exported is pink and far from exciting; the Dão region of central Portugal produces the best wines and the red wines are particularly good. In the Minho region in the northwest of the country the light *vinhos verdes* wines are produced on granitic soil; the red wines of Colares and the very sweet Moscatel de Setúbal are less well known.

Shellfish is excellent accompanied by a white *vinho verde* and the meat stews of the Galicia area, *cozidos* as they're called, are drunk with a red *vinho verde*. The red wines of the Dão go well with picnic *charcuterie*. Both *vinhos verdes* (young wines) and *vinhos maduros* (the mature wines) are wines for quaffable enjoyment rather than great occasions.

Australia

Many fine wines are produced in Australia but they are sold only in limited quantities in Britain. Best areas are the Hunter Valley, noted for its rich Burgundy Shiraz wines, and the Barossa Valley in South Australia, famous for its Rhine Riesling and red Cabernets.

Because the Australian table wine industry is of comparatively recent vintage (until the late 1950s more fortified and dessert wines were produced than dry beverage wines) wines are still made in European styles and it is quite easy to substitute Australian wines for the wines of Germany or France. With seafoods, fish, melon and salads try the young Rhine Rieslings and Riesling/Hocks. Cold chicken and ham go well with the mature Hunter and Great Western whites and the wines made in the Moselle and Sauternes style can be taken with fruit and pastries and puddings. The pink wines made from the Grenache grape are ideal with light summer dishes. The young reds from

OPPOSITE *Elmham Park 1977 was made by Robin Don, a Master of Wine, from grapes grown on his Norfolk estate at Elmham. He has seven acres of vineyard with a preponderance of Müller-Thurgau and Madeleine Angevine. A typical Elmham Park wine is light, dry and grapey with a fresh flavour which expands in the mouth and lingers on the palate. It goes particularly well with seafood, cold meats and salad, and is a perfect accompaniment to York ham.*

Eden Valley, Clare, Tahbilk and Coonawarra match pâtés, terrines, roast chicken, pasta, lamb and cream cheeses; the big mature reds are excellent with roasts and game.

South Africa

Best known for 'sherries', the Republic is beginning to export more and more wine, particularly the Chenin Blanc and Steen wines. There are 14 designated areas entitled to the title 'Wines of Origin' and there are also some 40 designated estates. Much experimentation is in progress.

The warm climate of South Africa has made the production of dry white wines extremely difficult but the Chenin Blanc and Steen are good all-purpose wines to be drunk whenever light white wines from Germany or the Loire would be appropriate. The red wines made from the Cabernet and Syrah grapes take their place happily with meats and cheese.

England

English wines are a comparatively recent innovation although the tradition of planting vines is said to go back to Roman times, when the climate was much hotter. The uncertain summers produce wines of high acidity which have to be fermented with added sugar but at blind tastings on the Continent they have done well when put up against comparable wines from Alsace and Germany. Only white wine can be made really well; there is seldom enough sustained warmth to ripen red grapes. The principal grape varieties are Müller-Thurgau, Seyval Blanc, Reichensteiner, Schönburger and Rieslaner. There are now nearly 200 vineyards in England and Wales, mainly in the south, and the wines are growing yearly in reputation. They are, many of them, pleasant light table wines which form a perfect accompaniment to the less substantial meat dishes (chicken, veal, ham, charcuterie) and to seafood and salads. Ideal drunk on their own on summer days, they are appearing increasingly on the wine lists of the more discriminating hotels and restaurants. They will never achieve mass-production, dependent as they are upon the vagaries of the English summer and to my mind will never become anything more than an interesting eccentricity.

California

Although vines have been grown on the west coast since the nineteenth-century the explosion in wine production and the creation of really excellent wine is a recent phenomenon. Experimentation is producing new hybrids and new vinification techniques and it is often difficult to keep up with developments. In the past California was noted for its mass-produced jug-wines and sweet fortified dessert wines but serious wine-makers are now producing excellent fine wines which are beginning to be drunk and enjoyed more and more in Britain.

The most popular red wine grape is the Cabernet Sauvignon, followed by the Zinfandel and the Pinot. Among the white the Chardonnay, Johannisberger Riesling, Emerald Riesling, Fumé–Blanc and Gewürztraminer all produce wines which are markedly different from their European counterparts. Two popular pink wines are a pink 'Chablis', medium-sweet with some sparkle, and a slightly sweet *vin rosé* made mainly from the Grenache grape. Wines are also produced in other parts of the United States but it is to California which importers in Europe will be looking in the future and we shall undoubtedly be seeing more and more excellent wines from the Napa Valley in particular.

Many Californian wines are made from grapes of only one variety and it is quite simple to partner them with appropriate foods as long as one buys them for their varietal characteristics.

Wine with Food·2

Although many wines, particularly white wines, can be enjoyed and appreciated without even a cheese straw to help them down, the finest wines of all, the great red wines of Bordeaux and Burgundy, need the added dimension of food to reveal all their virtues; they are 'table wines' in the true (though not the legal) sense of the word. It is the addition of wine that raises food to its greatest heights.

A skill in matching wine with food demands slightly more than a facility for balancing the liquid with the solid. We've seen how wines can vary from light to full-bodied; from dry to sweet; from weak to strong. Food has similar degrees of substantiality, from light salads and vegetable dishes, undemanding white fish and chicken through to solid fare like roast meat, game and pies and puddings. There are similar nuances when it comes to desserts: every gradation from the delicacy of sorbets and simple fruit salads to concoctions rich in carbohydrates and cream.

There are, let's face it, many foods which don't go with wine at all. These are better on their own or accompanied by some more suitable beverage. Eggs, for instance, rich in sulphur, just don't seem to be happy with any wine except when they are blended in sauces or prepared *à la bourguignonne* with red wine. Smoked food is difficult to partner with wine. What would you drink with kippers for instance? Better to leave these highly aromatic foods on their own. The Scandinavians have a similar problem with all their herring specialities marinated in vinegar or salted and spiced. Here the only appropriate

OPPOSITE *Wine with soup is perhaps too much of a liquid delight but a dry Madeira or a pale dry fino sherry goes well with a consommé or that classic cold Spanish soup, gazpacho. There is no reason why you shouldn't take a glass of red wine with a minestrone or a game soup. Suggested here is a fine Australian Metala. Big and rich, the wine is blended from 40% Cabernet Sauvignon and 60% Shiraz. Aged in oak and bottle, the bouquet is perfumed and the wine is of great depth. If you're having a strong meaty soup, then the bigger the wine the better.*

drink is either lager or akvavit. Similarly a salad which has been dressed heavily with malt vinegar in the English fashion is death to wine: the two should never be confronted.

The palate and organs of smell are sensitive and delicate but they can easily be confused and misled. A wine which seems thin and tart at the first sip can slowly change as your tastebuds adapt to it. I have seen a blindfolded whisky blender mistake a glass of water for a glass of Scotch after a prolonged tasting. So the palate should not be overwhelmed at any time. If you are going to eat a dish in a piquant or spicy sauce then a mild Mosel will be bowled over and completely neutralized. On the other hand a mild dish can be spoiled by matching it with a wine so big that it ousts all other sensations from the mouth.

If you bite a slice of cooking apple after a bar of chocolate you will find the fruit unacceptably sour; take the same apple after sucking a lemon and it will be sweet in comparison. Taste is subjective and it pays to take wine in a logical order of progression.

On the apple and chocolate principle never serve a sweet wine before a dry, or if you do, allow time for the palate to recover; otherwise the dry wine, however mellow, will taste sharp and acid by contrast. As with a well-planned firework display, keep the best and most dazzling wine to the end. Any modest wine served after a really good one will seem coarse, thin and inferior in comparison: serve the cheap wine before the more expensive and the young before the mature. And for these same reasons don't follow a full red wine with a dry light white; that would be like eating bread after cake.

There is no need to serve more than one wine with a meal but if you have eight at the table two different wines will provide a more interesting menu. Three will make it even more of an occasion. If you do serve only one wine then it is perhaps safest to choose a rosé or a medium-dry white. With chicken, turkey, pork or veal this would be very acceptable, but few people enjoy drink-

ing white wine with a roast or a casserole. Many expect a glass of red wine with their cheese. Choosing to serve only white wine throughout will definitely limit your choice of food.

The very best picnics I've had while travelling through Europe have been accompanied by white wine (ideally cooled in a convenient stream) drunk with sliced sausage, smoked ham, some shellfish perhaps, grapes, peaches, bread. Red wine, however light, is often too soporific in the heat of the day. It is on a picnic that pink wine comes delicately into its own, ideal with the light, easily digestible food that the prudent person would prepare for a midday alfresco meal.

There are a very few people who will actually create a meal round certain outstanding wines, but most of us instinctively choose the food and then desperately look around for something not too unsuitable to go with it. And it's the main course that will probably determine which wine we are going to spend the most money on. If the main course is going to be rich and highly flavoured then the wine must be able to stand up to it and not be knocked for six. A powerful wine is called for with a pigeon stew. Put a weak little rosé up against a steak and kidney pie and it will faint with fright on your palate; similarly a light and elegant Mosel will not do well with roast beef. And the reverse is true. You don't want to stifle a delicate plate of sweetbreads with a robust red wine. Always avoid clashing tastes at the table in the same way that you would avoid incongruous colours in the dining room.

Avoid, too, anything which gives you no pleasure. Even the cheapest bottle of wine is an expensive item; drinking something because you feel you ought to rather than because you want to is foolish. A great deal depends on the environment in which you are drinking your wine. I lived in the tropics for many years in the days when not every restaurant was air-conditioned and our own dining room sometimes reached a humid 95°F. even with the fans turning overhead. I seem to remember enjoying

white wines far more than red. Rhône wines or Shiraz wines from Australia were often far too overpowering for that sweltering heat.

People often talk about wines not travelling well. In the old days that meant that many wines suffered physical changes during a long sea voyage because they hadn't been stabilized against extreme changes of temperature. In these days of refrigerated filtration and high-speed sterilized bottling most medium-quality wines will travel happily anywhere without being noticeably impaired.

What I mean by a wine not travelling well is something very different. That little rosé wine drunk at the beach restaurant in August in the south of France was absolutely right with crudités, shellfish and salad. I brought a couple of bottles home and in the back garden on a windy London day it tasted very thin and uninteresting. The wine probably hadn't changed one bit; the difference lay in the contrasting environments. It was a question of atmosphere, and the wine hadn't 'travelled' at all well. I can think of many food and wine combinations enjoyed abroad that somehow just don't survive the transition to an alien clime.

When considering which wine to serve with a particular kind of food it is important to realize that a raw material

can be completely altered by its form of presentation. Thus a wine which would be suitable with roast chicken might be most unsuitable for curried chicken, chicken in cream sauce or chicken pilau. A lightly poached flounder needs a light wine but grill the fish and smother it with anchovy sauce and you will need something stronger.

Perhaps more than any other food, fish demonstrates the need for flexibility when it comes to choosing an appropriate glass of wine. I would drink dry crisp white with my fish by preference but I have noted over the years that many Frenchmen order red wine, especially with salmon – which they regard as a 'fat' fish whose oiliness needs something like a Beaujolais to stand up to it. Not to my taste but certainly to theirs and one more confirmation that rules are made to be abandoned at the pull of a cork.

Finally, always remember that, as they say in the North, 'you don't get owt for nowt!' If you are only prepared to pay small amounts of money for your wine you will generally be offered the cheapest and the most indifferent. If you are going to spend a fair bit of money on food then it deserves the best wine you can afford to go with it. Ill-made wines will not enhance good food. The finer the food the more it will show up nasty wine.

Starting the meal

Soups and broths are curiously difficult to partner with wine. A glass of sherry or Madeira goes well with a consommé or broth; a fish soup could be served with a manzanilla or a Muscadet and a heavy game soup made of hare or venison would logically go with a glass of port or big red wine. With cold soups like gazpacho, vichysoisse or cucumber, one could easily drink a fino or manzanilla, a dry apéritif wine from Montilla, or a full-bodied Riesling. But is it strictly necessary? If a food doesn't demand wine then perhaps it is best left unaccompanied.

This rule, as I have suggested earlier, should certainly apply to any hors d'oeuvres which contains brined or pickled fish, smoked herring fillets, eel, smoked oysters, shrimp or prawn cocktail. These dishes are difficult if not impossible to improve with a wine. If you do want to serve one then it should be white and of the right weight to stand up to the taste sensations involved. Soave, Muscadet, Verdicchio, Graves, Alsace Sylvaner, Entre-Deux-Mers, Pouilly-Fumé, Chablis, Dão, Vinhos Verdes, Mâcon-Villages, Gewürztraminer or a Californian or Australian Riesling are all possibilities.

There are some first courses which without question kill wine stone dead. I'm thinking of grapefruit, egg mayonnaise, avocado vinaigrette or anchovies. With melon, however, you could easily serve a glass of sweet sherry or a tawny port.

If you are the sort of person with enough money to buy Beluga caviar or smoked salmon then you will undoubtedly drink Champagne with it; with your oysters you will take Chablis, dry Graves, Muscadet, a Chenin Blanc from South Africa or a dry sparkling wine.

What other rules about starters? Meaty pâtés and terrines demand a red wine; fish pâtés and mousses and fish soufflés need a white wine. There are some ambivalent pâtés (chicken liver, for instance) which would go equally well with red or white. Where the rules dissolve themselves is at a buffet when guests are left to choose whether they will drink red or white wine. Some will

OPPOSITE AND LEFT *Picnics are a good occasion for white and pink wines, better still if you can find a nearby stream in which to chill them for a while.*

WINE WITH FOOD

The chart on these pages provides a very rough guide to what kinds of wines go well with what foods. Use it as a basis for experimenting yourself. A separate chart for cheeses appears on page 97. For a guide to wines which fall into the taste categories shown here, see page 35.

	White wine						Rosé (pink)				Red wine					Sparkling wine			Sherry	Madeira	Port
	Bone dry	Dry	Medium dry	Medium sweet	Sweet	Very sweet	Bone dry	Dry	Medium	Sweet	Light & fruity	Light & dry	Medium	Medium – full-bodied	Full-bodied	Dry	Medium	Sweet			
First Courses																					
HORS D'OEUVRES																					
Oil & garlic based		•	•																•	•	
Cream & butter based		•	•																•	•	
Smoked meats and salami		•	•				•	•	•		•								•	•	
Smoked fish		•	•	•													•		•	•	
Fruit based				•	•	•											•		•	•	•
PÂTÉS & TERRINES																					
Fish	•	•	•	•			•	•	•												
Game		•	•								•	•	•	•	•						
Meat		•	•	•							•	•	•	•	•						
EGGS																					
Soufflés, fish	•	•	•				•	•													
Soufflés, cheese	•	•								•			•	•	•						
Omelettes & quiches	•	•	•							•			•	•							
SOUPS																					
Consommé																			•	•	
Fish	•	•	•	•															•		
Broths		•	•																•	•	
Velouté		•	•																		
Cold summer soups	•	•	•	•	•		•	•	•										•		
Hot creamy soups	•	•	•	•			•	•	•												
PIZZA, PASTA & RICE																					
Tomato & garlic													•	•							
Fish/chicken	•	•	•				•	•	•		•	•	•								
Meat											•	•	•	•							
Cream sauces		•	•																		
Fish																					
WHITE FISH																					
Plain	•	•	•													•					
Grilled/fried	•	•	•																		
Cream sauces		•	•	•				•	•												
SHELLFISH & CRUSTACEA																					
Mussels, clams etc.	•	•	•										•			•	•				
Lobster, crabs	•	•	•				•									•	•				
SALMON, TROUT etc.	•	•	•	•												•	•				
MACKEREL, HERRING etc.	•	•	•																		
Poultry																					
Roasts/grilled	•	•	•	•	•		•	•	•		•	•	•	•		•	•				
Boiled	•	•	•	•							•	•	•	•	•	•	•				
Stews & sauté	•										•	•	•	•	•	•	•				

	White wine						Rosé (pink)				Red wine					Sparkling wine			Sherry	Madeira	Port
	Bone dry	Dry	Medium dry	Medium sweet	Sweet	Very sweet	Bone dry	Dry	Medium	Sweet	Light & fruity	Light & dry	Medium	Medium – full-bodied	Full-bodied	Dry	Medium	Sweet			
Game																					
Roasts													•	•	•						
Stews													•	•	•						
Meat																					
BEEF																					
Boiled								•			•	•	•	•	•						
Roasts/grilled											•	•	•	•	•						
Stews & sauté											•	•	•	•	•						
Cold	•	•	•				•	•			•	•	•	•	•						
LAMB & MUTTON																					
Chops/roasts												•	•	•	•						
Stews/boiled/sauté											•	•	•	•	•						
MINCED (BEEF OR LAMB)																					
Hamburgers							•	•			•	•	•								
Chili con carne		•	•				•	•			•	•	•								
Moussaka							•	•			•	•	•								
PORK & HAM																					
Chops/roasts	•	•					•	•			•	•	•	•	•						
Boiled	•	•					•	•			•	•	•	•	•						
Stews & sauté	•	•					•	•			•	•	•	•	•						
VEAL																					
Roasts	•	•	•	•							•	•				•	•				
Sauté	•	•	•	•							•	•									
Cream sauces	•	•	•	•							•	•									
OFFAL																					
Mixed grill											•	•	•	•							
Kidneys											•	•	•	•	•						
Sweetbreads												•	•	•	•						
Oxtail												•	•	•							
Tongue	•	•	•	•							•	•									
Tripe			•	•	•						•	•									
Hearts											•	•	•	•							
Desserts																					
FRUITS																					
Soft fruits			•	•	•					•								•			
Others	•	•	•	•	•	•										•	•	•			
CREAMS, CUSTARDS & ICES			•	•	•																
CAKES			•	•																	
ENGLISH PUDDINGS																					
Fruit			•	•	•													•			
Milk																				•	

start with white and move to red; others will stick to one or the other. Watching what people do drink when left to their own devices confirms that some people don't like red wine and some don't like white wine; and some, sadly, don't notice much difference either way. However I'm assuming they won't turn up to eat with you too often.

Fish

In general the stronger the fish (turbot, halibut, skate) the bigger the wine you will need to match it or overcome it. I'm not suggesting that wine and food should ever be seen to be fighting for survival when confronted with each other but sometimes presenting unlikely combinations can create a conflict. Smoked salmon and scrambled egg might well be served with a light young claret; it would certainly be interesting. And on the principle that a sweet white wine – a Vouvray, a Coteaux du Layon, or a Sauternes – is happy with *pâté de foie gras* you could certainly try a sweetish Deidesheimer spätlese with fish in a rich cream and butter sauce. Sylvaner, Gewürztraminer and Riesling wines go well with trout but again it depends how the fish is cooked. An all-purpose wine like a Mosel is an excellent choice with a *truite au bleu*, the fish cooked plainly and served with melted butter.

Wines that partner shellfish naturally (crab, lobsters, mussels, clams and scallops) include Alsace Riesling, Gewürztraminer, white Burgundies, Rheingau, Graves and Entre-Deux-Mers. Bone-dry rosé wines would do equally well, and the white wines of the Loire are particularly suitable: Sancerre, Savennières, Pouilly-Fumé and any wine made from the Sauvignon Blanc grape. Don't forget other wines such as Bourgogne Aligoté, California Chardonnay and Gros Plant from the same region as Muscadet.

I have been talking as if one should really only drink white wine with fish. It is certainly true that fish with red wine can create a ferrous taste in the mouth but there are many delightful exceptions. One of the best fish parties we ever gave was accompanied by red wine. We made a *bourride* (fish, onions, tomatoes, garlic, saffron) and as there was no white wine in the house we drank *vin rouge* with it. The garlic which might possibly have killed a white wine worked splendidly with the rough red Midi.

OPPOSITE *There is something particularly propitious about the marriage of Muscadet with seafood. The Muscadet vineyards, which lie next to the mouth of the Loire, produce a pale, light, fresh wine which has an almost salty taste of the sea. To the southeast of Nantes are the vineyards between two small rivers, the Sèvre and Maine, which give their name to the finest of the Muscadets. This bottle from the Domaine de l'Hyvernière is* tirè sur lie, *drawn off the lees (see page 119) and the wine has a liveliness and prickle that complements both bass and fennel.*

ABOVE *This young pink Domaine de Féraud, an appellation* wine *from the Côtes de Provence, is dry yet fragrant, and makes an ideal accompaniment to Bouillabaisse, the classic fish soup which is really a stew. Onions, tomatoes, garlic, olive oil, fennel, parsley, thyme, saffron with briskly boiled crustacea and fish – a perfect Mediterranean feast.*

There are of course plenty of classic French fish dishes prepared with red wines – *lamproie bordelaise, morue enrayte, sole bourguignonne, saumon Chambord, Matelote de meunier, sole au vin rouge, matelote d'anguilles, meurette à la bourguignonne, sole ménagère* to name but nine – and it is fitting that if the fish is cooked in red wine then red wine should accompany it. And preferably the same wine: Chambertin with *Sole au Chambertin* if you can afford it. That economical fish stew of Marseilles, *bouillabaisse*, is usually drunk not with white wine but with rosé de Provence, a wine produced locally in abundance.

The traditional fish dishes of the French classical cuisine are based all too frequently on ingredients which are not readily available outside France – and if they are (oysters, salmon, sole) are frequently so expensive that it seems a pity to do anything other than enjoy them as simply as possible. But there is no reason why the cheaper varieties of fish shouldn't be used far more. Try angler or monkfish which tastes delectably like lobster; blue ling, an excellent substitute for cod; rock salmon; saithe; dab; John Dory (another taste-alike for lobster); and witch. We tend to be far too unadventurous in our cooking. In England we give whiting (the Americans call it silver hake) to the cat. But just look what the French do with whiting. They cook it with white wine, shrimps and oysters; they poach it, stuff it, grill it and treat it like royalty. And if *Merlan frit en lorgnette* sounds much more enticing than fried whiting that's probably because the French have ways to make you hungry!

Meat

Ideally, especially in the summer, cold meats are best served with dry or medium-dry white wines or pink wines. The meat here is unlikely to be strong and light fruity wines can be served equally well. With cold pork pie, game pie or any pie made of red meat choose red wine, the best you can afford: Bordeaux, Loire, Burgundy or from further afield.

With roast chicken and turkey reds are pleasant but white is in order. But if the birds are heavily stuffed only the really big white wines like Burgundy can compete; it's safer to stick with red. A guinea-fowl stuffed with haggis (to bring more flavour to this factory-farmed bird) needs a weighty red wine.

Try Chianti, claret, Cabernet Sauvignon, Rioja, Fronsac, Bourg, Rhône, Barolo, California Burgundy, Corbières or Mâcon Rouge.

Duck and goose, being rich and fat, call for big wines; whether red or white depends on your own personal preference. Most people would settle for a red Burgundy or Bordeaux or a Rhône wine, an old Chianti, a New World Zinfandel or a Shiraz from Australia. Try, too, the big German wines – Rheinpfalz Spätlese, for instance.

Strong game, hare, venison and wildfowl demand the biggest of red wines and certainly these be found everywhere from France to Argentina. The Germans, who have no such abund-

ABOVE *Duck calls for a rich wine, white or red. We've chosen a fruity and readily acceptable claret from St Emilion which has been called the 'Burgundy of Bordeaux'. Château Bon Prince is neither one of the 11 premiers grands crus classés, nor one of the 70 grands crus classés. The 1973 was, however, awarded a grand cru distinction which would not necessarily appear on a 1974 label.*
OPPOSITE *With Greek food like kebab and salad, choose a Greek wine. The one shown here is from the Peloponnese, made from a blend of Mavroudia and Aghiorghitico grapes. A wine unique to Greece is Retsina, which derives its distinctive aroma of varnish from the pine resin used in fermentation. Usually white, Retsina is loved by some and hated by many.*

ance of red wine, consider that their Spätlese and Auslese wines go with almost anything. And the richest white wines, those of the Palatinate and Rheingau, are habitually drunk with red meat and game.

Meats like pork and veal are traditionally paired with white wine but light red and full whites are equally good. Riesling, Graves, Hock, white Valdepeñas, Valpolicella, Frascati – the list is endless. With ham choose red or white depending on the recipe; if the ham is baked with a sweet sauce a pink wine would perhaps be best of all; if it's baked with a Madeira sauce why not serve Madeira?

White wine is seldom a success with beef. You should opt for red wine, of the best quality you can afford. Beef is not cheap and the wine should not be cheap either. Burgundy is ideal but look to Italy, Eastern Europe, South America and California for other excellent choices. For lamb the wines can be lighter but still red; claret or its equivalent or a light Beaujolais. Lamb stew calls for something more robust. Grilled steaks, kidney, liver and sausages also need a red wine, though not one of the same finesse that a sirloin of beef commands.

Cheese

It is the custom in most wine-drinking countries which also have a dairy industry to serve cheese before the dessert. This enables your guests to finish whatever red wine they may have in their glasses before moving on – should they be so invited – to the pudding. If you have only served white wine with the meal then the order of dessert and cheese is academic. Indeed it might be more logical to serve the dessert first and then offer cheese with a glass of red wine or port. Much the most sensible decision is to put the cheese on the table and allow people to make their own decision.

There is an old saying in the wine trade that you should buy on an apple and sell on cheese. The palate is sharpened by an apple and is better able to appreciate the imperfection of a wine; cheese is kind to wine and in particular a full red wine. Hence the

English love affair with port and Stilton.

A recent tasting organized by the English Country Cheese Council and the Wine Development Board scored with the following combinations:

Caerphilly – *young dry white German wine*
White Wensleydale – *dry white Frascati*
Red Leicester – *claret*
Double Gloucester – *Beaujolais*
English Cheddar – *red Italian Barbera*
Sage Derby – *Alsace Traminer*
New Lancashire – *sherry*
Blue Wensleydale – *Cyprus Commanderia*
Blue Stilton – *port*

The French, in addition to producing

the greatest red wines in the world, also produce the finest cream cheeses – there are nearly 250 different regional variations made from goat's, ewe's and cow's milk. A good restaurant may offer 10 or more varieties on its cheese board; some are soft, some blue-veined, some semi-hard. When in France it is a sensible choice to drink the local wine with the local cheese; they are bound to go well together. Strong cheeses need a full-bodied wine, milder ones go better with a light wine. But these are only generalized rules, made to be broken depending on the wine you have available. The table on this page gives a few suggestions for partnering French cheeses with French wines.

Soft paste with flowery rind Brie, Camembert, Carré de Bray, Chaource, Neufchâtel, Pyramide, Valençay	**Light red wine** Beaujolais, Bergerac, Bordeaux-Médoc, Bourgeuil, Chinon, Corbières, Corsican wines, Mâcon Rouge, Minervois
Soft paste with washed rind Livarot, Maroilles, Munster, Reblochon, St-Florentin, Vacherin	**Full-bodied red wine** Burgundy, Cahors, Coteaux du Languedoc, Côtes-du-Rhône, Pomerol, St Émilion
Soft paste with naturally formed crust Banon, Charolles, Morbier, Olivet, Picodon, Pont l'Évêque, Rocamadour, St-Benoît, Vendôme	**Dry white fruity wine** Alsace, Anjou, Pouilly-Fuissé, Sancerre
Processed cheese Crème de Gruyère, Fondu aux Noix, Fondu au Raisin	**Dry white or rosé wine** Arbois, Clairette du Languedoc, Corsican wines, Costières du Gard, Coteaux d'Aix-en-Provence, Côtes de Provence, Mâcon Blanc, Mâcon Rosé, Muscadet, Pouilly, Rosé d'Anjou, Saumur, Savoie, Tavel
Veined cheese Bleu d'Auvergne, Bleu de Bresse, Fourme d'Ambert, Roquefort, Saingorlon	**Full-bodied red wine or sweet white wine** Anjou, Barsac, Jurançon, Monbazillac, Sauternes
Semi-hard cheese Cantal, Gaperon, Laruns, Murol, St-Nectaire, St-Paulin, Savaron, Tomme de Savoie	**Full-bodied red wine** *see above*
Hard cheese Beaufort, Comté, Gruyère de Comté	**Dry white or rosé wine** *see above*

OPPOSITE *Red wine is generally better with cheese than white. In the foreground, Camembert; in the background, fromage aux noix, Tomme au raisin, dolcelatte, red Windsor and Cheddar.*

A HOME TRUTH.

Host (sotto voce). "IS THIS THE BEST CLARET, MARY?"   Mary (audibly). "IT'S THE BEST YOU'VE GOT, SIR!"

Desserts

It is here, at the end of the meal, that the sweet wines come naturally into their own. The fruity quality wines of Germany are a good choice, but you should also consider the sweeter champagnes (*sec*, *demi-sec* and *doux*) and sparkling wines like Asti Spumante, the sweet Tokays of Hungary, the famous fragrant and sweet Monbazillac wine produced from vines grown on the slopes of the Dordogne, the naturally sweet wines of the Loire such as Quarts de Chaume and Bonnezeaux, the Christian Brothers' Château La Salle, and the wines of Sauternes and Barsac. Marsala, Malmsey and Malaga and the sweet oloroso, cream and brown sherries, late vintage Alsatian wines, the *amabile* and *abboccato* wines of Italy and any wine from anywhere made from the Muscat or the Sémillon grape are other possibilities.

Be careful to consider whether your dessert actually calls for a wine. Rhubarb and custard, chocolate ice cream and tinned fruit all spring to mind as dishes that positively discourage it. Wine can also be wasted on tart fruits served in certain ways: buried in a rich *patisserie*, apple might go exceedingly well with a sweet wine from Orvieto, but a crisp Cox's Orange Pippin eaten on its own requires, if anything, only a glass of port. On the other hand that superb English winter pudding Sussex Pond, in which the centrepiece is a whole lemon surrounded by suet pudding, becomes so subtly flavoured that Madeira or any sweet sparkling wine would work wonders with it. The really expensive sweet wines are best left to dominate the end of the meal either on their own or with an innocuous sweet ripe fruit.

ABOVE *An awkward moment at the dinner table. One of Du Maurier's popular* Punch *cartoons poking fun at the social pretensions of the day.*
RIGHT *A nineteenth-century Bohemian goblet with elaborate overlay. Decorated glasses obscured the impurities in sweet German wines, and were very popular until this century.*
OPPOSITE *Crêpes suzettes and strawberries call for something sweet and rich and there's nothing richer than a fine Sauternes. In 1975, only 18,000 bottles were made at Château d'Arche from the 36 hectares of vines. Gold in colour, the wine is honeyed and might well qualify upon occasion as nectar. Sauternes is best bought in half-bottles, as shown here; a little goes a long way.*

After the meal

Even if no cheese has been presented I cannot think of a better end to any meal in the autumn than a glass of vintage port or LBV with some green cobnuts or young green walnuts straight off the trees, rich in sap and as different from the kiln-dried variety as grapes are from raisins. Peeled of their skin and dipped in a little salt they are the ideal nutty partner to port.

Some wine merchants have been known to serve a slice of fruit cake with port after a meal. In Oporto at the elegant Factory House (factory as in

OPPOSITE An English tradition which is hard to beat: port, here a Late Bottled Vintage, and Stilton.

BELOW These four glasses have one feature in common – the rim curves inwards to retain the bouquet, which is one of the prime pleasures of drinking Cognac. The bowl is palm-shaped for warming in the hand and to allow you gently to eddy the spirit so that it releases its aroma. Glasses with bowls the size of footballs are ideal for displaying chrysanthemums, not Cognac.

'factor' not industrial plant) there are two long dining rooms, each a mirror replica of the other. Both have identical tables and it is customary after the meal for the guests to move from one room to the next and take their places at the second table where almonds, walnuts, brazils and fresh and dried fruits are waiting to be tasted with a selection of the finest vintage ports in the world.

Port ought always to be served at room temperature and although vintage port should be consumed on the day it is opened most ports will keep for some time after opening but not indefinitely. Prolonged exposure to the air is no better for good port than good sherry. The most appropriate sherries for drinking after a meal are the olorosos and amorosos.

Many people enjoy a glass of Cognac or Armagnac after a fine meal. These, or any other brandies should not be served in huge balloon vases. Neither should the glass be heated over a naked flame – that is a vanity which ought to be

confined to pretentious expense-account restaurants. Warm the glass in the palm of your hand and savour the aroma as it ascends, that is all that is needed.

Marc (pronounced *mar*) is a distillation of the grapeskins, stalks and pips left over from wine-making. Like brandy it is made in many countries and has a markedly pungent taste which you either like intensely or find most unpleasant. The best-known marc comes from Burgundy but it is also distilled in Champagne, Alsace, Burgundy and the Loire. Like any other distillation it improves with ageing in oak and it can mellow to a very fine drink indeed.

Wine in the Restaurant

There are very few restaurants which employ a professional *sommelier*, that is, a waiter who really knows the contents of his cellar and has an excellent idea of which wine to suggest to accompany any dish on the menu. In Britain there is a Guild of Sommeliers whose members are encouraged to learn about wine, visit vineyards, attend lectures, pass examinations and eventually become extremely knowledgeable about wine.

If you come upon one of these wise and educated men throw yourself upon his superior knowledge. Tell him what you propose to eat and seek his advice. If he is a skilled sommelier he will tactfully find out what your particular taste in wine is and how much you're prepared to spend. He should then be in a position to suggest two or three wines which might appeal both to your pocket and your palate.

If he can see that you are unable to make up your own mind he will discreetly coax you towards a decision: 'May I bring you a bottle of the Hermitage sir? It's very reasonable, one of our better Rhône wines and I think it

will go beautifully with your steaks. As a matter of fact I had a glass myself at lunchtime and it was really first-class. I don't think you will be disappointed.'

And of course with a build up like that how could you be disappointed? But I'm afraid that kind of sommelier is one in a hundred. Even in France it is only in the starred establishments that you will find an enthusiast in charge of the wines and even then you may find yourself in the hands of a man motivated more by selling the most expensive than the best.

Imagine my joy on a recent visit to San Francisco to find a sommelier in the Clift Hotel who was an expert on Californian wines. On my first visit I think I talked, or rather listened, more than I ate, but here was a man who knew his vineyards and his vintages and, more importantly, knew the condition of the wines in his cellar. 'No, no, no!' he said on one occasion when I thought I'd try a particular wine. 'What you want with the fish is a Robert Mondavi Fumé Blanc. You taste that and you'll know how good our Napa wines can be. It's in

the style of the upper Loire wines and has the real aroma of the Sauvignon grape.'

At least he said something along those lines and we were swept up and into the meal by his delight in sharing our delight at well-made wine partnered with good food. I suppose I could recount the number of times I've encountered that degree of expertise on the fingers of one tired hand. Usually the wine waiter is a member of that stage army of itinerants who go from restaurant to restaurant learning very little but the latest fiddle and the easiest way to pass an evening with the minimum amount of work.

Then again you may come across advice which is downright unhelpful. I have been offered Liebfraumilch with a beef stew and rosé with osso bucco. And it's not only in Britain that knowledge of wine is sketchy. The export manager of a Cognac firm, a Frenchman with a very sophisticated taste in wine, told me how once in Toronto a waiter approached his party, who had ordered steaks, and said breezily: 'What would you fellows like to drink? Like a nice wine with the steak? How about a Drambuie?'

In a Birmingham hotel (England, not Alabama) my host chided the waiter gently for not bringing the wine until we were halfway through the main course. The excuse was so gnomic and memorable that I repeat it in full: 'Well sir, you see it was like this. I could see you were a man of taste, sir, and I didn't want to bring the bottle too soon in case it got cold on the table!' A remark equalled only by the waiter in a Hull hotel who once said to me with great pleasure: 'I hope the wine's all right; as it's a cold night I put it on the hotplate to warm up.'

I have on at least one occasion witnessed the opposite thermal cruelty. In a Soho restaurant a waiter brought a bottle of Liebfraumilch to a nearby table, astonished the party with a

LEFT *A wine connoisseur – slightly the worse for wear – sizes up a dessert wine. A cartoon from* Punch.

103

glimpse of the label which depicted some jolly blonde mädchen disporting in front of a fairy-tale Rhine castle, uncorked the wine and tried to pour some into a glass. Alas, it was frozen solid. Which brings us back full-cycle to the hotplate.

I relate these stories, all of them true, so that you may take your courage in both hands when eating out, confident that wherever you go it is unlikely that your knowledge of wine will be as sketchy as the waiter's.

Not infrequently a waiter will hand you the wine list and stand gazing into space while you leaf through anything from 40 to 200 wines depending on the seriousness of the restaurant. Either send him away until you're ready to order, or try to seek his advice. If you know what you want to drink it is simple to turn to the appropriate section and select a suitable bottle. But there are many wine lists which feature unusual wines and you should always look through the whole list in case there is a bargain tucked away in some remote corner. It could come from Chile, Hungary, Bulgaria or Argentina and may well be a better wine than some dubious example from the classic French regions. Learning how to spot that bargain is, I'm afraid, a matter of trial and error.

Today it is not uncommon for a hotel to have wines on its list from a dozen different countries but the majority will almost certainly come from France. The list will start with vintage and non-vintage Champagnes from perhaps a dozen or more of the big houses.

Then there will be the red wines of Bordeaux ranging from the simple regional wines through the lesser growths to the great names of the Médoc, St Emilion, Pauillac, St Julien and Pomerol. These great wines will be high-priced and should always be decanted before they are to be drunk. For most of us, they are reserved for real celebrations, and you should choose them only when you have complete trust in the restaurant. Ideally they should be ordered in advance so that they can be brought to the dining room and given a chance to reach if not mouth temperature at least room temperature.

The white wines of Bordeaux range from dry Graves to sweet Sauternes but it will be the white wines of Burgundy, full in flavour and rich in bouquet,

These two illustrations appeared in the French magazine Le Rire *in 1904 as 'the myth . . . and the reality'. Left, the boisterous nature of New Year's Eve in Paris, as imagined by those in the provinces. Right, how the Parisians sedately spend that evening.*

which will be the most expensive. These are wines which reach their peak between three and six years after bottling and which are ideal with fish, chicken and veal.

The white Burgundies will include such names as Chablis, Corton-Charlemagne, Meursault, Puligny-Montrachet, Chassagne-Montrachet, Bâtard-Montrachet and the great Montrachet itself, all made from the Chardonnay grape. There will also be wines from the Côte Chalonnais and the Côte Mâconnais including among the latter the famous Pouilly-Fuissé.

The red Burgundies, which mature more quickly than clarets and may well be better value, will be next on the list. Better to drink a young Burgundy which probably isn't going to improve much after six or seven years in the bottle than

a young claret which may well not have reached its peak.

The red Burgundies (Gevrey-Chambertin, Clos de Tart, Chambolle-Musigny, Clos de Vougeot, Echézeaux, Vosne-Romanée, Richebourg, Nuits St Georges, Corton, Pommard, Volnay) will, if they are from reputable shippers, and of outstanding years, be very expensive and again if you are paying large sums of money for such wines you are entitled to expect that they have been cellared with care and will be handled and decanted with expertise.

Then follow the wines of Beaujolais (white and red) and the Côtes-du-Rhône and more famous names: Fleurie, Brouilly, Moulin-à-vent, Morgon, Juliénas, Crozes-Hermitage, Châteauneuf-du-Pape. It is likely that the wine list will then move on to wines from Alsace, the Loire, Provence and Jura before arriving at the white wines of Germany – Nahe, Rheinhesse, Rheinpfalz-Palatinate, Rheingau, Franken and Mosel-Saar-Ruwer. After that you are likely to find wines from Italy, Switzerland, Austria, Hungary, Spain, South Africa, Australia, Portugal, California, England and other countries.

Many restaurants confine themselves to a few house wines and such well-established favourites as La Flora Blanche, Blue Nun, Goldener Oktober, Golden Guinea, Mouton Cadet, Mateus Rosé and generic Sauternes, hocks and Burgundies.

In addition to the complexity of individual wines there is the hurdle of vintages. Should one order a 1975 or a 1972? There are various pocket-sized charts published for enthusiasts which one can whip out furtively when the wine waiter isn't watching. If you think such lists are worth consulting (bearing in mind that even in a great year many vineyards will not necessarily make great wine) have a look at the list on this page. Even in the poorest years there are individual triumphs so one shouldn't put too much reliance on vintage charts. They are like crossword puzzles; they give infinitely more pleasure to those who compile them than to those who have to cope with them.

One other advantage of knowing good vintages can be put to use when reading a wine list. If you want to choose a medium-priced wine but are unfamiliar with those listed, look to the great wines for guidance. If you see, say, a Bâtard–Montrachet from an excellent year, you'll have good reason to trust the rest of the list; if, however, the great wines listed are from the not-so-great vintages, be cautious about the rest of the list.

If you are accustomed to buying wine retail or even wholesale you may well be horrified at the mark-up to be found in restaurants. A £3.00 bottle of Côte Rotie may well be selling at £7.50; a £2.20 Niersteiner Gutes Domtal could be on the list at £5.60. In Britain restaurateurs have long been accustomed to using wine as the jam on the bread (they make only a modest profit on their food) and they will explain that having a considerable amount of their capital tied up in the storage of a wide range of wines is expensive. That money must be recouped.

The average mark-up can range from 50 per cent to 150 per cent; in France, where the tax on wines is so low as to be negligible, a restaurant may well charge 300 per cent and not excite comment. However high you find the price of a bottle of fine wine in a restaurant in Britain you will almost certainly pay far more for it in France.

When you enter a restaurant be sure that you are given the wine list as early as possible. There is an illogical arrangement in many places which leaves the food waiter and the wine waiter acting independently, with the result that your food may well appear on the table before you have a chance to order anything to drink. Never allow food to be placed on the table before the wine has appeared; if you do you will almost certainly find that you have eaten it before the wine arrives or, equally depressing, find that you are drinking your white wine with the meat and your red wine with the coffee.

If the wine waiter knows nothing about his wine list pick your own way carefully through it. First you must decide whether you are going to have both white and red or just stick to one wine. With a large party it is easy to please everyone, even if some order fish and others meat; even with two people it is possible to have half a bottle of white followed by a half-bottle of red. And, of course, there's always rosé. Most restaurants will also sell you wine by the glass so that if you have chosen white wine you can also have the pleasure of a glass of red with the cheese. It will not be a fine wine but it should be an honest drinkable wine. The practice of selling sweet wine by the glass to drink with dessert is on the increase.

Always pick the wine you want to drink, never the wine you think will impress the waiter. Wines are usually arranged within their categories in an ascending order of price, and many people believe that the wine the restaurant wants to get rid of is always placed second on the list. (Few people will order the cheapest, many will settle for the second cheapest.) Don't be deterred from doing what you think is right; in your case it *is* right.

The professional wine waiter will never force expensive wine on someone who really wants a modest bottle nor will he force red wine where white is wanted. According to one master sommelier: 'I'm very happy to find a red or white wine to go with any dish; what really makes me cringe is when someone asks you to mistreat a fine wine. I remember being asked to put a superb claret, a really outstanding St Emilion, in the ice bucket. I did of course. The customer is always right. But it upset me deeply!'

Never upset a good wine waiter; place your trust in him and he will guide you to the right bin – the right one for *you*. One of the advantages of eating in a good restaurant is that you can usually order your wine by the carafe or half-carafe, confident that if the establishment has a good wine list they will not ruin their reputation by buying 'rotgut' as a house wine. If it's not a very good restaurant, be wary; many house wines are undrinkable. Always ask what the house wine is before ordering it.

The *Good Food Guide* for 1979 exposed a team of inspectors to 11 red and 10 white wines most frequently bought by restaurateurs as their carafe wine and they found the results were disappointing. Only three of the 21 wines were judged 'very good'.

Once you've chosen a wine the waiter should bring the bottle you have ordered to the table and show it to you. This is not to impress you with the picture on the label or the shape of the bottle; it is to make sure that he has heard your order correctly. If you have

The cellars of an old established London restaurant. Its 2000 bottles of wine include 13 different clarets, 18 different burgundies and 15 splendid ports to accompany the Stilton.

asked for Château Pathé you do not want to be drinking Château Pavie at twice the price. Check, too, that if you have ordered a wine of a particular vintage the wine presented is of that year. If it is any other year then an explanation should be given. The bottle should never be opened before it is first brought to the table; the only exception to this is house wine, whether in bottle or carafe.

If the wine is red then it should not be ice-cold. Feel the bottle. If the wine is white the waiter will either bring it chilled or place it in an ice bucket to cool it. The custom of bringing red wine to

the table in a wicker basker is a silly convention which should be politely discouraged. The cradle was invented so that a wine butler could move a very old bottle of wine from the cellar to the place of decanting with the minimum amount of disturbance to the sediment. The elaborate rigmarole with which many waiters surround the opening of an ordinary bottle of red wine with no deposit or sediment is designed to impress you, not to improve the taste of the wine.

However the waiter is not always entirely to blame. There are far too many restaurants frequented by people with more money than good sense who demand a three-act drama every time they order a bottle of wine.

If you want your wine to be decanted, ask the waiter to do this. If you want the wine to breathe, ask that the bottle be opened as soon as it is brought to the table – though this is fairly standard practice nowadays. When the waiter does open the bottle he will offer the host a sample taste. This is not an affectation because there is always the possibility that there is a flaw in the wine. Only by smelling and tasting it can you be sure

A wine waiter from Hendschel's Sketchbook, *published in the 1890s.*

that it is fit to be drunk. Again, the exception is house wine, where you will not often be offered a taste before it is poured.

The occasions on which you may have to reject a bottle will be few and far between. With modern techniques of bottling the wine should be in good condition, but just as you may occasionally find a mouse in a milk bottle so a wine may be unacceptable. If the cork has crumbled while being withdrawn there may be a few slivers floating in the wine. This is really no excuse for demanding that the wine be taken back. The alert waiter will notice this kind of thing himself and will remove the pieces. A pinhead or two of cork in the wine should not be confused with a 'corked' wine. Corked, or spoiled, wine is rare; it smells of rotten wood and comes from a defect in the cork itself. It is more than likely that you will pass through a life-time of wine-drinking without encountering a corked wine.

If you think that there is something wrong with the way in which the wine has been brought to the table (a white wine too warm, a red wine too cold) then you must bring this to the waiter's attention. What he does then is up to him. It is not uncommon for a waiter to remove a bottle which is not acceptable and then five minutes later bring it back with an apologetic flourish saying: 'Try *this* one sir, I think you will notice the difference.' The wine game has many diversions for the uninitiated; even the ritual tasting of the wine is regarded by the pompous as an occasion for almost religious concentration.

When it comes to the pouring a well-trained waiter will only half-fill your glass; filling it to the brim robs you of the pleasure of smelling the bouquet, eddying the wine about to bring it back to life after its long entombment in the dark and generally contemplating its virtues. I once had my glass filled so full that short of asking for a straw there was no method of conveying it to my lips without spilling it. Frequently you may find it more satisfactory to pour the wine yourself. The constant replenishing of half-emptied glasses gets through bottles at a gratifying rate (for the restaurant) but can become a nuisance. A fussing waiter is worse than no waiter at all.

There are a few restaurants which are unlicensed and carry no wine list but allow you to bring a bottle with you.

You may be asked to pay what is known as 'corkage' for this, but the charge is generally a nominal one.

Lunching or dining out should be fun; as long as the service is reasonably good, don't spoil the occasion yourself by being too demanding, or let others spoil it for you. If the wine is a little too warm make allowances; if the waiter is rushed off his feet possess yourself in patience. Eating out should also be an excuse for exploring new wines. If you only ever order standard branded wines that you've drunk a dozen times before then you are not likely to widen your wine horizons and you are not the sort of person who will be reading this book. You will like what you like.

For those who are prepared to be adventurous my advice is to equip yourself with a reliable guide to restaurants and choose only those which are run by people interested in both wine and food. You will be able to rely on their advice with confidence.

Buying Wine

It has been estimated that the growing of vines and the making and marketing of wine provides a living for 37 million people. For some of them it is a very marginal living indeed; for others the life–style is luxurious. Somewhere along the line between the planting of the vine and the opening of the bottle all sorts of people are adding their labour and expertise and many others are taking their hefty percentage from the bottle of wine you drink.

Their number includes the person who grows the grapes and the person who makes the wine – not always one and the same; the buyers and shippers; the wholesalers and finally the retailers – shopkeepers and restaurateurs. Add to this the costs of bottles, labels, corks and capsules, advertising, and it's not surprising that wine is not a cheap commodity.

And we haven't finished yet. In Britain, in the USA and in most countries which import wine various taxes are levied. It all mounts up. The less you pay over the counter for a bottle of wine the more you are paying for the overheads. If you pay £1.25 for a bottle of *vin ordinaire* the actual value of the wine in the bottle may be as little as 12p – in other words nine-tenths of your purchase is not drinkable. But pay a little more and see what happens. If you buy a £2.50 bottle it is likely that the real value of the wine in the bottle is around 90p. So you are getting seven or eight times more quality in your wine.

Although it pays to shop around when you are buying wine it seldom pays to spend as little as you possibly can. The very cheapest wine *tastes* cheap and frequently nasty (thin, tart, acid) and that's because it frequently *is* cheap and nasty. Made to stringent business margins from the most inexpensive bulk wine available, the wine is drinkable, but only just.

The most heavily advertised wine is not necessarily the best. Because everyone orders it, you do not necessarily have to follow suit. The history of the rise of branded wines in Britain is an interesting one. Before stringent labelling regulations came into force it was very easy for an importer to buy cheap wine by the tankerful and blend it to suit the taste of his customers. What they put on the labels was, after all, nothing to do with him. If they wanted wine labelled Châteauneuf-du-Pape, Nuits St Georges, Beaune or Chablis then he would concoct as zealously as he could something which resembled such wines. He might be mixing Algerian wine with French, or Italian with Spanish, all in a lucrative if not a particularly honest cause.

Today, even with the rigorous EEC regulations, deliberate fraud is still a temptation. The heavily regulated wine trade in France stands or falls on its Appellation Contrôlée (see pages 54–7); when, in 1973, it was revealed that a long established firm had perpetrated an elaborate fraud to cheat the law by topping up AC wines with inferior wine, a *frisson* of horror ran round Bordeaux. Wines from the Midi, the inspectors alleged, had been passed off as wine from the Gironde. It emerged in evidence that half the wine produced in France's most productive wine-growing area of Languedoc-Roussillon found its way to Burgundy and Bordeaux to reappear under the more lucrative labels of those two premier wine regions.

With all the rules in the world, you cannot be perfectly sure that the wine in your bottle is everything it claims to be. Particularly if it is claiming high quality at a ridiculously low price. More than half the wine we drink in Britain is blended and sold under nationally advertised names.

These wines may vary in both price and quality but they do contrive to produce a desirable taste, flavour and, most important, consistency from year to year. This is not always achieved, and they can vary significantly depending on the origin of the wine in the bottle. There was a scurrilous canard going the rounds not so long ago based on the provenance of one large brewer's branded white wine. The tanker–lorry bringing it, so the story went, began its journey in Yugoslavia and filled up as cheaply as possible in every country it passed through. And that may not be so far from the truth. When a wine buyer is shopping to a budget and in bulk he must go where the best bargains are. On the other hand the emergence into the wine–trade of big supermarket groups and chain stores has in many ways raised the quality of branded wine. Applying rigorous quality control and buying in huge quantities, they can generally guarantee the consistency and value of their wines.

In the last decade wine clubs, discount warehouses, cash-and-carry centres, cut-price liquor marts and small retailers specializing in wines from particular regions have proliferated. Competition is fierce and this has led to a great deal of price-cutting. Offices and institutions have set up their own wine-buying co-operatives, auctions are well attended, national newspapers have gone into the bargain-offer business. Wine has become extremely easy to buy.

Shopping around can yield excellent bargains; it can also fill your cellar with rubbish. Wine magazines and newspaper wine columns can keep you abreast of the world of wine; just remember always that a very low price usually means not much value.

If you have suitable storage space, consider buying wines to 'lay down', that is, to lie in your cellar (or possibly under the stairs) until they have aged and are ready for drinking. You will have to pay more for these wines – many of the lower- and medium-priced wines don't improve with age – but by the time you drink them they may well be worth three or four times what you originally paid.

It is also worth remembering that if you are only going to buy one bottle of wine at a time you are losing the possible discount advantage of bulk purchase. Discuss your long-term requirements with a knowledgeable wine merchant and he will be only too pleased to advise you how to buy ahead to beat inflation and have finer wines for drinking than you could afford without such foresight. He may even be willing to store it for you, in more reliable conditions. In a

ABOVE AND LEFT *Two contrasting styles of purveyors of wines – inside a large multiple store and the window of a small independent retailer.* RIGHT *Your choice at the wine merchants. From left to right, 2 litres, 1½ litres, 1 litre, standard 75cl bottle, and a ½ bottle. Fine wines are rarely sold in the three larger sizes, though many acceptable grades of wine are.*

time of inflation and rising fiscal duty it is obviously good sense to buy now and drink later.

Many wine merchants organize tastings at which an expert, usually a Master of Wine, will take a small group through a range of wines of a particular region or varietal origin. These are not to be confused with tastings organized by merchants only anxious to dispose of as much wine as possible. The Wine and Spirit Education Trust organizes courses and examinations throughout Britain and its activities are backed by the combined muscle of the Worshipful Company of Vintners and Distillers, the Masters of Wine, the Wine and Spirit Association and the Wine Development Board.

Many local education authorities organize day and evening classes in wine appreciation and it should be easy to find out from the local library or directly from the Wine and Spirit Education Trust (Five Kings House, Kennet Wharf Lane, Upper Thames Street, London EC4) what facilities for learning are available in your own vicinity. Or why not organize tastings of your own? Half-a-dozen people is enough to form a club, and you can enjoy extending your knowledge of wine in the company of good friends.

A growing number of hotels and restaurants now mount special 'gastronomic' dinners featuring the wine and food of different regions with both chosen to complement each other. There are also more ambitious food and wine weekends organized by a number of hotels and these will include tastings and lectures and excellent opportunities to meet others who are interested in the pleasures of food and wine. The International Wine and Food Society, which has branches throughout Britain and all over the world, organizes tastings and dinners for its members, which are again an excellent opportunity to learn more about the pleasures of the table.

Wine and Health

If you enjoy drinking wine it is relatively easy to find chapter and verse to prove that it is a beneficial food. As a distinguished French professor once put it: 'A litre of wine contains one-eighth of our nutritional requirement and nine-tenths of good humour.'

And I like the good Dr Shaw's praise of wine: 'Drunk in moderate quantities wine has a power to give sudden refreshment, to warm the stomach, gently stimulate its fibres, promote digestion, raise the pulse, rarify the blood, add to its velocity, open all obstructions, forward excretions, greatly promote insensible perspiration, increase the natural strength and enlarge the faculties both of body and mind.' And given time it might well re-paper the dining room and mow the lawn as well!

There are no less than 155 references to wine in the Old Testament, most of them complimentary, and who would knowingly go against the advice of Holy Writ? There is no doubt that, in moderation, wine can be extraordinarily good for you. Medical men tell me that it contains, in small quantities, calcium, chlorine, cobalt, copper, iodine, iron, magnesium, phosphorus, potassium, sulphur and zinc – and we all know how vital such things are for a full and happy life.

If you need riboflavin it is more stimulating and interesting to obtain it from wine than from cornflakes. The presence of vitamins A, B and C in wine is a welcome bonus. Over the years there have been plenty of doctors who have been happy to point out the efficacy of individual wines – no doubt in return for a crate or two for their own personal researches!

The anti-bacterial properties of wine were particularly important in the days of endemic typhoid and wine has been recognized as an antiseptic since biblical times. The great Francatelli, chef to Her Majesty Queen Victoria, was quite convinced that indispositions could be alleviated by a glass or two of the appropriate wine. 'For instance,' he wrote, 'a person of sanguine temperament feels a necessity for a light sapid

wine, such as genuine Champagne and Rhenish wines, while the phlegmatic seek those of a more spirituous, generous nature, Burgundy, port, Madeira or sherry ... In short, Burgundy is exciting, Champagne is captious, Roussillon restorative and Bordeaux stomachic.'

What splendid nonsense, but of course how true. The placebo effect of wine should not be dismissed out of hand. Port has traditionally been prescribed for invalids and the French, who take their health very seriously, attach as much importance to the therapeutic quality of wine as they do to mineral and spa waters.

As a sedative, a specific against gallstones, piles, diarrhoea, cholera and many disturbing conditions too upsetting to name, wine in small quantities can do no harm.

I must confess, having been a wine and food correspondent for a leading medical journal for many a year, that I have never visited a wine-producing area which hasn't been able to summon striking evidence, usually at professorial level, that drinking the local wine is far better than a visit to the doctor.

In northeast Hungary, where they make the top quality wines of Tokay, I was told that this wonderful wine was stocked in Hungarian pharmacies until 1934 and that Austrian chemists recently isolated penicillin within its rich and warming interior.

Dr E. A. Maury, a respected graduate of the Faculté de Médecin de Paris, claimed that while in practice as an acupuncture specialist and homeopathist he had an impressively high success rate treating his patients with wine. Indeed in a fascinating book he paired particular wines to particular ailments, but he was careful to point out that wine should be drunk in conjunction with food.

Dr Maury analyzed wines for their acid and tannin content and, more importantly, their mineral composition, and he was able to prove to his own satisfaction that some wines appeared to be indicated for specific ailments. The Médocs were beneficial, he found, for

anxiety, lack of appetite, diseases of the bronchia, coliform infections, depression, diabetes, enteritis, pregnancy, rickets, salmonella, tonsilitis, tuberculosis, typhoid and urticaria. Champagne mitigated fever, phosphate loss, hiatus hernia, sluggishness of the stomach, and coronary disease. Were you a follower of Dr Maury you would drink Sancerre for gout, the wines of Provence for obesity, Côtes du Rhône for influenza, Vouvray for dyspepsia, Gros Plant for urates, Alsace for abdominal flatulence and Anjou for cystitis!

Dr Maury is a bit of a loner in these matters and doctors have long since abandoned wine therapy in favour of ethical drugs. But it is still true to say that few doctors would dissuade their patients from having a glass of wine with a meal even if it were one of the proprietary 'tonic' wines fortified with sodium glycerophosphate, aneurine hydrochloride, caffeine, niacin, potassium iodide, malt, meat extract and other unlovely-sounding substances. The one ingredient that all tonic wines have in common is a fair amount of alcohol and they may well induce a temporary alcoholic euphoria if consumed in large

Calories per 100ml (4 fl oz)	
Apéritifs	
Sherry, dry	120
Sherry, medium	140
Sherry, cream	160
Vermouth, extra dry	140
Vermouth, white	200
Vermouth, red	180
Table Wine	
Dry white	80
Dry red	80
Sweet white	100
Sparkling Wine	
Dry	60–70
Medium-dry	75–85
Port	160–200
Tonic Wines	160–200

SANTÉ SOBRIÉTÉ

ne vous laissez pas prendre au piège: on peut être alcoolique sans être jamais ivre

Schoumann

enough quantities. But, as one doctor told me, 'If you really feel run down the place to go is not the wine merchant but to the doctor!' Taking to the bottle when you're feeling below par can lead to a pattern of addictive drinking and the fact that the drinking can be disguised as medicinal is potentially dangerous.

Most tonic wines claim that they will cheer you up but they are invariably extremely unpleasant and over-sweet. Some taste of metal polish, others are bitter. Best to spend your money on natural wine, not these fortified 'medicines'.

There are all sorts of folk myths about wine which medical research has proved to be unfounded. It used to be thought that the excessive drinking of port induced gout. Now we know that it is a function of the metabolism of uric acid and gout can affect teetotallers as well as wine–drinkers.

Wine is of course a food. Food is fattening. There is no such thing as a slimming food. An average wine is

two-and-a-half times as strong as beer but one-fifth the strength of spirits. Dry red and white wines contain fewer calories and less carbohydrate than an equivalent amount of very sweet wines, but within that framework there is a wide variation in the strength of wines. Many wines are quite low in alcohol. The light Mosels, for instance, have only eight centilitres of alcohol per litre of wine while some big red wines may be up to double that amount in strength.

Diabetics should be careful with wine. Dessert wines and fortified wines should as a general rule be avoided, although the occasional glass of port, sherry or Madeira, if watched in relation to the rest of the food intake, is acceptable. The British Diabetic Association points out to its members that the German Wine Institute has introduced a yellow seal of approval which indicates a dry wine with not more than four grammes of residual sugar. With this low sugar content, the wine is ideal for diabetics in *small* amounts. They also recommend the still

Alcoholism is alarmingly high in many western countries, including France where the government has launched a forceful campaign to combat it. This poster, linking health and sobriety, warns 'Don't let yourself be trapped : you can be an alcoholic without ever being drunk'.

wines of the Coteaux Champenois, both red and white, which have an unusually low carbohydrate content.

For those who are keen slimmers it should be remembered that all alcoholic drinks have a high Calorie or Joule value; the calories derive from the alcohol. The chart on page 113 gives some idea of the calorie intake from a range of grape-based alcoholic drinks. From a chart like this you can establish quite easily that a bottle of Burgundy would be about 630 calories and a bottle of light Mosel might be about 520 calories. As part of a calorie-controlled diet wine can be incorporated into the daily regime in the same way that bread and potatoes can – with discretion. Consumed in excess wine can be as fattening as anything else rich in calories.

Glossary

Acidity If a glass of wine is so tart that it purses your lips then it is probably afflicted with a surfeit of acidity. Acids occur naturally in the grape itself. A wine lacking acidity is bland and flat; a certain amount of acidity, particularly in white wine, is essential to give that fresh, sharp taste one associates with such wines as Muscadet and Sancerre. Wine-makers welcome tartaric and malic acid in their wine; acetic acid turns wine to vinegar. Generally speaking, the more sunshine a grape sees, the lower its acidity will be. Yet English wines, however sunny their south-facing slopes, tend to be high in acidity; wines produced in hot countries like Spain and Italy tend to be lower in acidity. Balance is all.

Aftertaste The sensation of wine which remains in the mouth after swallowing. The greatest wines leave a long lingering farewell in the throat; unfortunately, the nastiest do the same.

Ageing Many wines are made to be drunk young and are none the worse for that. Keep a wine too long in wood and it may well become old and tired. All table wines improve in bottle but most are not going to get appreciably better after the age of three or four; by five years old they may well be over the top. On the other hand there are many Bordeaux wines which when young are hard and harsh and do not reveal their full potential for a decade or more. As a rule of thumb white wines are usually drunk younger than red wines, with the exception of the great classic Burgundies and the sweet wines of Bordeaux and Germany.

Alcohol Enzymes secreted by yeast cells convert grape sugar into ethyl alcohol during the process known as fermentation. Table wines contain from 8–16 per cent of alcohol. Fortified wines can be as strong as 22 per cent.

Apéritif Literally an appetizer, a drink offered before a meal to stimulate the tastebuds and arouse the desire for food.

Appellation Contrôlée A French wine bearing the letters AC or AOC should be a guarantee that the wine in the bottle has been produced according to certain rules administered by the Institut National des Appellations d'Origine (INAO). The types of vines permitted to be grown, their acreage, yield and the way in which the wine has been made are all subject to regulations. This controlled system of production helps to produce *genuine* wine; it does not guarantee that the wine will taste good.

Aroma Some grape varieties like the Gewürztraminer (almost spicy) and the Muscat (highly perfumed) have very distinctive aromas. There are those who can detect the smell of raspberries, violets or blackberries in certain wines. These fruity scents tend to be more prominent in sweet wines than dry ones. The aroma is the smell of the grape; much of it can disappear during fermentation and ageing. It is noticeable that the driest wines have less aroma than sweeter wines which have not lost all their natural grape sugar. As a wine ages its aroma vanishes into the 'bouquet', that is, the smell that the wine develops as it ages in the bottle.

Astringent Wines which cause the mouth to pucker (as at the entrance of a lemon) are called astringent. They will probably have too much tannin in them; many will smooth with age.

LEFT *An old, dry white Saumur from the Anjou region of the Loire.*

Baked A term applied to wines made from grapes exposed to excessive heat and sunshine and minimal rain. They are mainly found in Australia, North Africa, Argentina, South Africa, California and parts of the south of France.

Bianco Italian for white. *Blanco* is the Spanish; *blanc* the French. The word 'plonk' is said to derive from the way the Tommies in the First World War pronounced *vin blanc*, which they were offered in French *estaminets*.

Big A term applied to a wine high in alcohol, full of flavour.

Blend The introduction into Britain of branded wines, some of which are very eccentric blends, has given rise to the suspicion that blending is in some ways underhanded. It must be remembered that all sherry and a great deal of Champagne, port and Madeira is blended. Mixing the produce of one vineyard with that of another can often enhance the wine and well-made blends should be accepted for what they

are: an attempt to produce a consistent product at a reasonable price. Bear in mind, too, that many great wines are the mixture of different grapes from a given vintage.

Body A wine with a high alcoholic content and plenty of tannin is often said to have body. Great clarets, when young, have more body than they need; with age they mature to a rounded perfection. Wines from sun-drenched parts of the world – Argentina, Spain, southern Italy – tend to have more body than wines from northern Europe. For a good example, compare a big Australian Shiraz with a delicate Sylvaner from Alsace: a heavyweight versus a bantam.

Botrytis Cinerea This fungus (known as 'noble rot' in English, *pourriture noble* in French and *edelfäule* in German) withers the grape, dehydrates it and concentrates the sugar, reducing the acidity and providing the basis for superbly sweet and honeyed wine. Tokay, Sauternes, Barsac, Anjou, Touraine and Germany all produce such wines.

Bottle Age The length of time a wine has spent maturing in bottle.

Bouquet Most wines which are made to age will, when opened, have a bouquet. This is a result of the wine's development in the bottle: the fruit, acids and alcohol will have oxidized to produce a scent that is quite distinct from the aroma of the original grapes. The finer the wine and the longer it has been in the bottle, the more likely it is to produce a pleasing bouquet.

Bourgogne A name which can be given to any wines made in the Burgundy region as long as they have a minimum alcoholic content of 10 per cent if red and 10.5 per cent if white.

Breathing 'Open the wine, waiter, and let it breathe, please.' I've heard that said about wines which need not air but the kiss of life. But most wines do improve after contact with the air and even a young wine is occasionally well served by being opened and decanted several hours before the meal.

LEFT *Sifting through grapes in the Douro Valley, Portugal.*

Carbonation Making wine sparkle by infusing it with carbon dioxide. In America such wines have to be labelled 'carbonated'; in France *gazéifié*. It seems a waste of time to adulterate wine in this way, even for fun.

Carbonic Maceration A technique which produces a wine of great fruitiness and intensity of flavour, suitable for early drinking. The grapes, in bunches, are placed in a sealed cement vat and fermentation occurs as the carbon dioxide is retained under slight pressure. This removes colour from the skins more quickly and the resultant wine needs a much shorter period of maturation. A technique popular in the Rhône and the Midi.

Cave The French name for a cellar. In Bordeaux, where there are few opportunities for tunnelling underground, the buildings where wine is stored are known as *chais*. In Jerez the warehouses are called *bodegas* and in Portugal *lodges*. In Champagne the wine is stored in galleries called *crayères*, which are carved out of chalk.

Chambrer To warm a red wine by letting it stand in the room in which it is to be drunk for long enough to let it acquire the ambient temperature.

Château A house (and it may be a castle or a humble home) which is part of a vineyard. The traditional name for a Bordeaux vineyard, the word château may not appear on a label unless there is

a vineyard attached to the property. Château-bottled means that the wine has been bottled on the property where it was produced – it guarantees authenticity if not quality. The French terms to describe a château-bottled wine are *Mis en bouteilles au Château* or *Mise du Château*.

Claret The term used originally in England to describe the light red wines of Bordeaux which the French dubbed *Clairet*.

Clos Literally an enclosure. A walled or enclosed vineyard as in Clos de Vougeot or Clos du Roi.

Corked A corked wine is one which has been spoiled by a rotten cork. It will

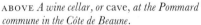
ABOVE *A wine cellar, or* cave, *at the Pommard commune in the Côte de Beaune.*

have a noticeable odour of dry rot or mushroomy dampness. The likelihood of your encountering a corked wine is remote.

Cradle A wicker or metal container which waiters brandish in pretentious restaurants. Few wines need this bath-chair treatment.

Cru Literally, growth. In the 1855 classification of the wines of Bordeaux, five growths (or divisions) of wines were established as *crus classés* (classed growths). These have since been revised from time to time, and today the use of *cru* usually means that the wine has come from a classified vineyard. *Crus bourgeois* indicates wines below the classed growths.

Cuve close The sealed–vat method of making sparkling wines.

Decant To pour wine from a bottle carefully and gently into a decanter or jug in order to separate the wine from any deposit or sediment that may have formed during ageing. A wine may also be decanted solely in order to aerate it and let it 'breathe' before it is consumed.

Deposit The dregs which form in the bottom of the bottle. In red wines this is

LEFT *A horse-drawn cart brings grapes from the vineyards at Chateau Figeac. Figeac is one of the* premiers grands crus classés *of St Emilion.*

ABOVE *English vines on the Beaulieu estate in Hampshire. The grape varieties which thrive best in England are the German ones; Müller-Thurgau in particular is widely planted.*

largely as a result of the decomposition of the tannin in the wine; in white wines tartrate is a more common deposit. Few of the wines we drink today 'throw a deposit', as it is called, but any that do (vintage port, some Bordeaux and Burgundies) should always be decanted before serving.

Demi-Sec Usually indicates a medium-sweet rather than a 'half-dry' wine.

Denominazione de Origine Controllata (DOC) Similar to the French AOC or AC, and introduced in Italy in 1963 to improve the quality of that country's wines.

Domaine French term for a wine estate, mainly used in Burgundy, The individual vineyards may be scattered in different townships or communes but as long as they are owned by one proprietor they remain part of his domaine. The wines will, however, be marketed under their separate *appellations* where appropriate. Estate-bottled wines bear the words *Mise du Domaine* or *Mis en Bouteilles du Domaine*.

Dosage A quantity of cane sugar dissolved in wine and added to Champagne or sparkling wine to give it the required degree of sweetness before it is finally corked for shipment.

Fermentation The process in which grape juice is converted into wine. Most wines undergo two fermentations. The first, in which sugar converts to alcohol, occurs immediately the grapes are put into the vats after picking; the secondary malolactic fermentation may not take place until the following spring.

Filtration Nowadays most wines are filtered to render them clear and bright before bottling. The filtering of wine through layers of asbestos has recently come under attack and is being discontinued; cellulose filter sheets are being used more and more. Over-filtration can rob a wine of much of its character.

Fining All wine contains floating particles when it is maturing in casks or vats. Fining is the introduction of other substances to carry the suspended particles down to the bottom of the cask, where they become known as 'lees'; white of egg, gelatine, casein, various forms of clay (usually aluminium silicate) or even fresh blood can be used. These fining substances then remain behind when the wine is racked off its lees.

Flor The Spanish word for 'flower', this is the white film which forms on the surface of certain sherries after fermentation. The flor yeasts make the superb finos of Jerez.

Flûte A tall narrow glass, cone-shaped and stemless, used for drinking Champagne; these days superseded by the tulip glass with its in-curving rim which retains the bouquet as well as the bubbles.

Fortified Wine Wines like sherry, port, Madeira, Málaga, Marşala and vermouth which have been strengthened with brandy or spirit.

Frizzante Italian term for slightly sparkling wine. (See pétillant.) The best-known frizzante is red Lambrusco, a fun, undemanding wine, frequently carbonated, which is popular in the US.

BELOW *Stainless steel fermentation vats at a château in Bordeaux. This is the stage of winemaking at which sugar is converted into alcohol.*

Fruity The attractive flavour of ripe grapes, found in young wines like Beaujolais.

Heavy A wine is heavy if it is more than 14 per cent in alcoholic volume; any wine below this is referred to as light.

Hock A term invented by the Victorians to describe Rhine wines, it used to apply only to wines from the Rheingau centred round the town of Hochheim. Today hock is used to refer to any table wine (*tafelwein*) from the Rhine region.

Litre A litre of wine is roughly equivalent to one-and-a-third standard bottles. One-and-a-half litres is equivalent to just over two bottles and the two-litre size is slightly less than three bottles. (A standard bottle generally contains 75cl.)

Lees The sediment left in the bottom of a vat or cask after the wine has been racked off.

Made Wines Wines produced in Britain from imported concentrated grape juice.

Malic Acid A fruit acid found in apples. During the malolactic fermentation malic acid in the grapes is converted into lactic acid. If too many unripe grapes are used, the wine may well taste of sour apples. Converting the malic acid into lactic acid renders the wine less tart and harsh.

Master of Wine In the early 1950s the Vintners' Company and the Wine and Spirit Association of Great Britain held the first examinations in wine theory and practice for members of the wine trade. Successful candidates are awarded the title of Master of Wine (MW); just over 100 men and women have passed since 1953. In 1980 the Institute of Masters of Wine assumed the responsibility for conferring this coveted award.

Maturation The process whereby the main elements in wine (sugar, acid, tannin and alcohol) combine and improve over a period of time in cask or bottle.

Medium–Dry A wine with some residual sugar present but dry enough to be enjoyed before a meal or possibly with food. Medium-sweet wines are too sweet for drinking other than on their own but not sweet enough to qualify as dessert wines.

Mis en Bouteilles Bottled. The label will say where: at the vineyard (château or domaine); in the region of origin; in the country of origin; or in the importing country.

FAR LEFT *Young grape vines on the sunny slopes of the Rheingau region in Germany.*
LEFT *These vineyards in the Ahr valley – the most northerly of Germany's wine-producing areas – are put under glass to protect them from an October frost.*
BELOW *Casks of Moët & Chandon Grand Reserve Champagne in the cellars at Épernay.*

Mousseux Foaming or effervescent. All French wines with a sparkle are known as *vins mousseux*; the exception is Champagne, considered too aristocratic to be demeaned in this way!

Must Grape juice or crushed grapes in the process of becoming wine. The French word is *moût*.

Négociant A French wine merchant who buys wine, looks after it, ages it, bottles it and ships it.

Noble Rot The mould which forms on the skins of ripening grapes (see *botrytis cinerea*).

Noble rot developing on a Riesling grape.

Non-Vintage A blended wine made from wines of different years.

Oenology The science of wine, its preparation and preservation.

Over the Top A wine past its prime. Many white wines, if kept for too long, can decline into an early senility. When buying bin ends it is wise to distinguish between those wines which may be on offer because they are left in small and non-commercial lots and those which are not worth drinking any more.

Oxidized The stale taste a wine gives off after prolonged exposure to the air. A white wine which has become oxidized will have a brownish colour and is described as maderized. Maderized wines are over the top.

Pasteurization The process of heating and sterilizing wines to destroy any unwanted micro-organisms and render the wines stable. Pasteurization hastens the ageing of the wine but it can also make it bland and uninteresting. Fine wines are not subjected to pasteurization.

Pétillant The French term for a wine which is slightly crackling or sparkling. The Germans use the word *spritzig*; we would talk about a sprightly wine.

Phylloxera The aphid which ravaged the European vineyards in the nineteenth-century. The only remedy which was successful in combating *phylloxera vastatrix* was grafting vines on to disease-resistant American rootstocks. Certain areas – Cyprus, Chile and California among them – were never plagued by phylloxera. Since the 1870s when the disease began to spread through French vineyards, there has been a debate about the difference between pre- and post-phylloxera clarets.

Primeur A young wine bottled shortly after the vintage. Apart from the most famous, Beaujolais, other primeurs on sale include the *vins de café* made by many Côtes-du-Rhône and Midi co-operatives, Muscadet and other Loire wines including Anjou, Saumur and Touraine. The Chianti producers also make a *vino novello* in November.

Racking The process of drawing off young wine from a vat or cask while leaving the sediment and lees behind. Wines are often racked several times before bottling.

Reserve A French word which is intended to imply that the wine is of superior quality. *Riserva* in Italy and *Reserva* in Spain, where on Rioja wines it is an indication of extra ageing.

Sec Dry, except when applied to Champagne. A 'sec' Champagne is medium-dry, an 'extra sec' is dry and a 'demi-sec' is medium-sweet. The driest of Champagne is labelled 'brut'.

BELOW *A wine press at work at Château Catius, near Langons in the Graves area of Bordeaux. The grape must is first collected in the trough and then pumped into a vat, where it will be left to ferment.*

ABOVE *Bottles of Champagne in* pupitres *at Veuve Cliquot in Rheims. The sediment is clearly visible.*

Sediment The natural deposit of crystals and solid matter that many wines develop as they age. White wines sometimes precipitate colourless cream of tartar crystals rather like granulated sugar – they are quite harmless.

Sekt The name for sparkling wine made in most wine-growing areas of Germany and varying in taste from sweet to dry. They are fermented mainly in glass-lined stainless steel tanks by the *cuve close* method developed in Saumur.

Servir Frais Serve cooled, not iced.

Sommelier The French term for a wine waiter who can be distinguished, in the more expensive restaurants, by his apron and his *tastevin* or tasting cup. A Guild of Sommeliers was founded in the UK in 1953 but the examinations are fairly stiff and internationally there are fewer than 40 qualified Master Sommeliers. The Society of Bacchus in the US is affiliated to the British Guild.

Sur Lie The technique of fermenting a wine, particularly Muscadet, on its lees gives the wine a definite prickliness and retains both its liveliness and fruitiness. If the wine is racked off its lees too soon before bottling it will oxidize and become flat. A Muscadet 'sur lie' is a wine that has been racked directly off its lees into the bottle, thus retaining its natural if small amounts of CO_2.

Tannin A group of organic substances found in the skins, pips, and stalks of grapes. They contribute to the maturing of red wines, which are richer in tannin than white wines. The more tannin a young wine contains the longer it will take to mature and, because the substance is a preservative, the longer it will live.

Thin A watery wine lacking body and depth.

Throw See deposit.

VDQS Vins Délimités de Qualité Superieure. A category created in France in 1949 for wines which did not quite come up to AC standards but which were considered to be a cut above the average.

VSO Very Superior Old, a blend of Cognacs older than most. VSOP means Very Superior Old Pale – even older Cognacs. There is, however, no legislation to lend authenticity of age to either of these designations. Like the stars on Cognac bottles, they dazzle but it's difficult to define them.

Varietal An American wine of premium quality made predominantly or completely from the grape variety after which the wine is called. The legal requirement is that 51 per cent of the

BELOW *Schloss Vollrads in the Rheingau. All the vineyards of this estate are in Winkel, about two kilometres to the south on the Rhine, but the estate's offices are in this castle.*

wine comes from the named variety of grape; many wine-makers use a greater percentage.

Vin de Paille White wine made in the Jura from grapes laid on straw in the sun. The grapes are full of concentrated sugar and yield sweet strong golden-coloured dessert wines.

Vin de Pays The lowest classification for French wines. Not all wine may be called *vin de pays*.

Vin Ordinaire Everyday table wine which the French drink by the litre, The Californian equivalent is jug wine. The legal definition of vin ordinaire is a superior table wine designation having regional identity.

Vinify To make wine from grapes. Vinification includes the whole process of wine–making from the crushing of the grapes to the filling of the bottles.

Vintage The year of the birth of a wine. The word is also used (*vendange*) to describe the period when the grapes are picked. In the northern parts of Europe where the weather is unpredictable vintages vary considerably from year to year; this is why some years are considered better than others. In hot southern countries there is less difference.

Vintage Charts These aim to provide an indication of good and bad years, but going by a year can be misleading. For example, 1977 was fair in Alsace, of low quality in Germany, adequate in Champagne, depressing in the Loire, excellent in the Rhone, disappointing in Bordeaux. There is no such thing as a universally good year, although 1959 came close to it.

Viticulture The science and art of growing vines and producing grapes.

Vitis Vinifera The indigenous European wine vine. The literal meaning is 'wine-bearer'.

Yeast Yellowish micro-organism found on grape skins which secretes enzymes that convert the grape sugar into alcohol. Wild yeasts are found in the air over every vineyard but specific yeasts are often artificially introduced into the must to aid fermentation.

ABOVE *Grapes ripening in the sun near Bologna in Emilia-Romagna, Italy.*
BELOW *A casual, friendly toast in the south of France.*

Vintage Chart

Vintage charts can never be more than a general guide to the broad relative merits of different years. Because of changes in climate and different wine-making techniques, to name just two of the factors that affect the quality of a finished wine, there are always exceptions to the lists. The best course is to become aware of the outstandingly good and particularly bad years; for those in between, it is likely to be a method of trial and error. This chart indicates the general quality of some French and German wines from 1965–1978. 1979 wines are only now becoming available, and are likely to be good if light, and soon drinkable; the 1980 vintage will probably be small for European wines due to the extremely wet, cold spring. Californian wines may fare better, despite the heatwave there.

The quality of a particular year is indicated by E (excellent), F (fair) or P (poor). The ageing required by wines of those years is indicated as follows: *ready to be drunk now; **can be drunk now, or further aged in the bottle; ***should be left in the bottle for a few more years to be drunk at its best.

	1965	1966	1967	1968	1969	1970	1971	1972	1973	1974	1975	1976	1977	1978
France														
BORDEAUX (RED) Médoc/Graves	P	E * **	F *	P	F *	E ** ***	F/E *	F *	F *	F * **	E ***	F/E ** ***	F ***	F/E ***
Pomerol/St Emilion	P	E * **	F *	P	P/F *	E ** ***	F/E *	F *	F *	F *	E ***	F/E ** ***	F ***	F/E ***
BORDEAUX (WHITE) Sauternes	P	F *	E * **	P	F *	F/E ** ***	F/E *	F *	P/F *	P	E ***	F **	P	F **
Graves	P	F/E *	F/E *	P	F/E *	E *	F/E *	F *	F *	F *	E * **	F/E * **	F **	F/E **
BURGUNDY Red	P	F/E *	F *	P	F/E * **	F *	F/E * **	F/E *	F *	P/F *	P	E ***	F ** ***	E ***
White	P/F *	F/E *	F/E *	F *	F/E *	F/E *	E * **	F * **	F/E *	F *	F *	F/E **	F **	F ** ***
Germany Moselle	P	F/E *	F *	P	F *	F *	E * **	P	F *	F *	E ** ***	E ** ***	F *	F * **
Rhine	P	F *	F *	P/F *	F *	F *	E * **	F *	F *	F *	E ** ***	E ** ***	F *	F * **

123

Further Reading

Strangely, while writing this book I hunted high and low for anything similar – partly out of curiosity to see how another writer might have tackled the subject and partly in the hope that I would find a few good pieces worth quoting. As far as I know there isn't any book currently available which concerns itself solely with the marriage between food and wine. There are however many excellent wine books, some of which allude to food, some of which don't. Here are the names of a few of the best:

The World Atlas of Wine Hugh Johnson (Mitchell Beazley 1971).
The Taste of Wine Pamela Vandyke Price (Macdonald and Jane's 1975).
The Wines of Bordeaux Edmund Penning-Rowsell (Allen Lane 1979).
The Wine Book Jancis Robinson (A&C Black 1979).
Encyclopedia of Wines and Spirits Alexis Lichine (Cassell 1979).
Wine Tasting Michael Broadbent (Cassell 1979).
Burgundy Vines and Wines John Arlott and Christopher Fielden (Quartet Books 1978).
Champagne Patrick Forbes (Gollancz 1967).
Sherry Julian Jeffs (Faber 1961).
Eating and Drinking in France Today Pamela Vandyke Price (Tom Stacey 1972).
The New Wine Companion David Burroughs and Norman Bezzant (Heinemann 1980).
Drinking Wine David Peppercorn, Brian Cooper, Elwyn Blacker (Macdonald and Jane's 1979).
Teach Yourself Wine Robin Don (EUP 1968).
The Wines of France Cyril Ray (Allen Lane 1976).
There is an excellent series of wine guides (*Bordeaux* and *Champagne* by Pamela Vandyke Price, *Burgundy* by Graham Chidgey, *Germany* by Hans Siegel, *The Rhône* by Peter Hallgarten and *Spain and Portugal* by Jan Read) published by Pitman.

Acknowledgments

The photographs in this book were supplied and are reproduced by kind permission of the following:
Anthony Blake 20, 21, 106
Cooper-Bridgeman Library 40 (bottom), 98 (bottom)
Daily Telegraph Colour Library 18 (Palomino), 26 (middle), 63, 64, 118 (top), 120 (right)
Mary Evans Picture Library 9, 15 (top), 98 (top), 103, 104, 105, 107
Virginia Fass 17 (Merlot), 62, 116, 117
Food from France 16 (Cabernet Franc & Chenin Blanc), 17 (Gamay, Gewürztraminer, Grenache), 18 (Muscat, Pinot Blanc), 19, 29, 115, 118 (bottom)
Hamish Hamilton/Mrs Helen Thurber 34
Image Bank 57 (photo Charles Staner), 110 (bottom © Bullatz/Lomeo), 122 (bottom)
Paul Kemp (see right)
Colin Maher 8, 12, 16 (Chardonnay), 17 (Müller-Thurgau), 18 (Pinot Noir, Riesling), 22, 25, 26 (top & bottom), 27, 47 (bottom), 58, 119, 120 (left), 121
Mander and Mitchenson 69
The Mansell Collection 11
Marks and Spencer Ltd 110 (top)
Ministry of Health, France 114
Picturepoint 28, 60, 122 (top)
Scala/Vision International 10
Sunday Times 33
Zefa 15 (bottom; photo J. Pfaff), 75

Designed by Sara Komar

Original photography by Paul Kemp (front & back cover, pages 1, 2, 4–5, 6, 13, 31, 32, 36, 38–9, 40–1, 42, 43, 44, 45, 46, 47 (top), 48, 50, 66, 67, 68, 70, 72, 73, 74, 76, 78, 79, 80, 82, 83, 84, 86, 88, 89, 92, 93, 94, 95, 96, 99, 100, 101, 102, 108, 111, 112)

Maps by Line and Line (pages 14, 54–5, 59, 61, 62, 63, 64, 65)
Illustrations by Ed Stuart (pages 24, 37, 45, 51)
Charts and tables by Peter Moore (pages 7, 23, 35, 38, 52–3, 56, 90–1, 97, 123)
The publishers would like to thank Les Amis du Vin for the supply of many of the wines for photography.

Index

Numbers in *italic* refer to illustrations. Maps, which have not been indexed, appear on pages 54–65.

acidity 115
aftertaste 115
ageing 115, 116
Aghiorghitico 94
aguardiente de crujo 13
Ahr 81, 119; *119*
air, exposing wine to 45, 116, 117
alcoholic strength of wines 22–5, 30, 65, 77, 114, 115, 116, 119
Alella 83
Aligoté 16, 71, 93
Alsace 17, 18, 19, 35, 39, 50, 54, 56, 71, 81, 89, 93, 97, 98, 101, 105, 113, 116, 122; *50*
Amarone 35
Ambassadeur 69
Amer Picon 69
Amtliche Prüfungsnummer 52, 58
Anjou 16, 34, 35, 39, 71, 113, 115, 116, 120
Antinori 71
apéritifs 30, 41, 67–73, 115
Appellation Contrôlée 49, 54–7, 109, 115, 121
Arbois 34, 81
Arkansas 65
Armagnac 30, 101
aroma of wines 33, 115
Arquebuse 69
Asti Spumante 18, 28, 35, 81, 98
astringency 115
Auslese wines 35, 52, 58, 81, 97, 98
Avignon 77
Ay 13, 26, 27; *26*

Baden 34
bagaceira 13
baked wines 116
Bandol 17, 77
Barbaresco 35, 81, 82
Barbera 16, 35, 81, 97
Bardolino 35, 81
Barolo 35, 81, 94
Barossa Valley 85
Barsac 25, 35, 77, 98, 116

Bâtard-Montrachet 104, 105
Beaujolais 16–17, 35, 39, 41, 56, 71, 73, 75, 77, 89, 97, 105, 119; *39, 74*
Beaulieu estate *118*
Beaumes-de-Venise 18, *71*, 77
Beaune 35, 56, 75, 77, 117; *76*
Beerenauslese, 35, 52, 58
Bellet 77
Bergerac, 35
bianco 116
big wines 116
Bishop punch 73
Black Velvet 69
blanc 57, 116
Blanc d'Anjou *see* Chenin Blanc
Blanc Fumé *see* Sauvignon Blanc
blanco 116
Blauburgunder *see* Pinot Noir
blended wines 27, 116
body of wines 116
Bonal 69
Bonnezeaux 35, 98
Bordeaux 8, 16, 17, 19, 21, 26, 34, 35, 49, 50, 54, 56, 57, 71, 75, 77, 79, 87, 94, 104, 113, 115, 117, 118, 120, 122; *50*
botrytis cinerea 19, 116; *120*
bottle-openers *see* corkscrews
bottle shapes 30, 50, 51, 54, 58, 60; *50*
bottle sizes 111, 119; *111*
bouquet of wines 33, 115, 116
Bourg 94
Bourgogne *see* Burgundy
breathing 116
Bristol Cream sherry 68–9
Brittany 15
Brouilly 17, 105
brut 28, 57, 120
Bual 30
Buck's Fizz 69
Bull's Blood 16, 75, 81; *74*
Burgundy 7, 16, 18, 21, 25, 34, 35, 39, 50, 54, 56, 57, 63, 65, 71, 75, 77, 79, 85, 87, 93, 94, 97, 101, 104, 105, 113, 114, 115, 116, 118; *50*
butler's friend, the 42
Byrrh 69

Cabernet 14, 16, 17, 34, 85, 87, 94; *16*
    d'Anjou 71
    Franc 14, 16, 35, 43; *16*
    Sauvignon 14, 16, 35, 85, 87, 94
Cahors 81
California 13, 16, 17, 18, 19, 29, 33, 34, 42, 65, 85, 93, 94, 105, 116, 122
calorie content of wines 113, 114
Campania 19

Campari 69
Canaiolo 14, 19
Cap Corse 69
carbonation 117
Cardinal punch 73
Carignan 77
Cassis 17, 19, 71, 73, 77
Castelli Romani, 35
Catalonia 17
cave 117; *117*
Cérons 35
Chablis 16, 18, 34, 35, 56, 65, 71, 73, 81, 89, 104
Chalon 16, 56, 77, 104
Chambéry 30
Chambertin 94
Chambolle-Musigny 104
chambrer 41, 117
Champagne 8, 13, 14, 16, 18, 27–9, 39–41, 43–5, 46–7, 49, 50, 54, 57, 65, 69, 71, 73, 78–81, 89, 101, 104, 113, 116, 117, 118, 119, 120, 121, 122; *27, 43, 50, 119, 121*
chaptalization 22
Chardonnay 13, 14, 16, 18, 19, 27, 34, 35, 75, 77, 85, 93, 104; *12, 16*
Chassagne-Montrachet 104
Château 57, 117
Château d'Arche, *99*
Château Bon Prince 94; *94*
Château Catius 120
Château d'Yquem 13, 19, 77–8
Château Figeac 117; *117*
Château La Salle 98
Château Lafite-Rothschild 13, 14
Château Latour 13
Château Margaux 33
Château Montelena 16
Château Mouton-Rothschild 16
Château Palmer 57
Château Petrus 17
Châteauneuf 14
Châteauneuf-du-Pape 17, 77, 105
Chauché Gris 19
Chavignol 81
cheese and wine 77, 78, 79, 81, 82, 85, 87, 97, 98, 101; *96, 100*
Chénas 17
Chenin Blanc 16, 18, 34, 35, 71, 79, 85, 89; *16*
Chianti 8, 14, 16, 19, 35, 50, 60, 65, 81, 82, 94, 120; *50, 82*
chilling wine 7, 37, 39–41, 45, 67; *6, 44*
Chinon 35
Chiroubles 17
Christwein 22, 58
Clairette 34

Clare 85
clarets 8, 14, 16, 45, 54, 65, 73, 75, 93, 94, 97, 104, 106, 116, 117, 120
classico wines 60
clos 57, 117
Clos de Tart 104
Clos de Vougeot 75, 104
cocktails 30, 69, 71–3
Cognac 8, 19, 29, 30, 39, 101, 121
Cointreau 73
Colares 85
colour guide to wines 38, 39, 40, 67, 68; *38–41, 67*
Commarderia 97
Coonawarra 85
Corbières 17, 94
corked wine 107, 117
corking 45, 54
corkscrews 42; *42*
Cornevent 16
Corton 104
Corton-Charlemagne 104
Corvo Bianco 35
cost of wines 105, 109
Côte de Beaune *see* Beaune
Côtes de Blaye 56
Côtes de Bourg 56
Côte d'Or 18, 71, 77
Côte Rotie 35, 105
Côteaux Champenois 114
Côteaux du Layon 16, 35, 93
Côtes de Luberon 78
Côtes de Provence *see* Provençe
Côtes-du-Rhône *see* Rhône Valley
Courvoisier 30
Crème de Myrtilles 71–3
cru 57, 77, 94, 117
cuve close 28, 65, 117, 121

Dão 35, 71, 85, 89
decanting 30, 45, 116, 117, 118; *45*
Deidesheimer spätlese 93
Delamain 30
Denominación de Origen 53, 63
Denominazione di Origine Controllata 53, 60, 81, 82, 118
deposit 45, 117–18
desserts and wine 79, 81, 82, 85, 90–1, 97, 98; *79, 99*
diabetics and wine 114
Dijon 71, 75, 77
distillation 29, 30; *29*
domaine 57, 118
Domaine de Féraud *93*
Domaine de l'Hyvernière 93; *92*
Dordogne 98
dosage 27–8, 118

Douro Valley 21, 28, 30, 63; *63*
Dubonnet 69
Duriff 19

eau-de-vie 13, 73
Échezaux 104
Eden Valley 85
Eiswein 35
Elmham Park 85; *84*
Emerald Riesling 19, 85
Emilia-Romagna 19, 81, 122
Entre-Deux-Mers 35, 56, 89, 93
Épernay 8, 27, 119
Eurocave, the 46

fermentation 22–5, 27, 28, 29, 30, 65, 71, 115, 117, 118, 119, 121, 122; *118*
Fernet Branca 69
filtration 118
fining 25, 118
fish and wine 75, 77–8, 81–2, 85, 89, 90–1, 93–4; *78, 92, 93*
Fitou 17
Fleurie 17, 105
flor 18, 118
fortified wines 29–30, 118
Franche-Comté 81
Franconia 50, 58, 81; *50*
Franken wines 35, 105
Frascati 35, 71, 97
frizzante 60, 118
Fronsac 56, 94
Frontignan 18
fruit and wine 73, 77, 78, 85, 87, 89, 98
fruity wine 35, 119
Fumé-Blanc 16, 19, 85

Galicia 85
Gamay 16–17, 34, 35, 41, 73, 77; *17*
game and wine *see* poultry
Gau-Bickelheim laboratory 22; *22*
Georgia 65
Gevrey-Chambertin 104
Gewürztraminer 17, 18, 35, 71, 81, 85, 89, 93, 115; *1, 17*
Gigondas 17
glasses, wine 37–9, 40, 98, 101, 118; *37, 40, 48, 98, 101*
grapes 13–19, 21–2, 27, 60, 116, 122; *12–19, 20, 21, 60, 116, 122*
grappa 13
Graves 19, 35, 56, 71, 77, 89, 93, 97, 104, 120
Grenache 17, 34, 35, 77, 85; *17*
Grey Riesling 19
Gros Plant 93, 113
Groslot 34

Harveys 68–9
heavy wine 119
Hennessy 8, 30
Hermitage 19, 35, 77
Hine 8, 30
hocks 16, 38, 65, 71, 85, 97, 105, 119
Hockheim 119
Houghton vineyard 63
Hungerford Hill vineyard 63
Hunter Valley 34, 85

Illinois 65
Inglenook 16

Jerez 8, 18, 29–30, 39, 49, 63, 67, 117, 118
Juliénas 17, 105
Jura 105, 122

Kabinett, 52, 58
Kir 71–3; *72*

labels, reading 49–65; *52–3, 64*
Lambrusco 81, 118
Languedoc 17
Languedoc-Roussillon 81
Latium 19
Latricières-Chambertin 75–7
lees 25, 93, 118, 119, 121
Liebfraumilch 16, 35, 41, 50, 51, 58, 71, 81; *42, 50*
light wine 119
Liguria 81
Lillet 69
Lirac 17, 71
Loire Valley 16, 18, 19, 25, 28, 34, 41, 54, 56, 71, 73, 93, 94, 98, 101, 105, 115, 122
Lungarotti wines 82

maceration, carbonic 117
Mâcon 16, 35, 56, 71, 75, 77, 89, 94, 104
made wines 119
Madeira 17, 29, 30, 65, 87, 89, 97, 98, 113, 114, 116, 118
Madeleine Angevine 85
maderized wine 120
Madiran 81
Main 58
Málaga 30, 35, 65, 98, 118
malic acid 119
Malmsey 17, 30, 98
Malvasia 14, 17, 19
Marc 13, 77, 101
Margaux 35
Marsala 29, 98, 118

Marsannay 71
Marseilles 75, 94
Martell 8, 30
Martina Franca 60
Mateus Rosé 49, 105
maturation 119
maturing 25–6, 28, 29–30, 46, 54, 82, 83, 116, 117
Mavroudia 94
meat and wine 75, 77–8, 79, 81–2, 83, 85, 87, 89, 90–1, 94–7; 76, 82, 94, 95
Médoc 16, 35, 56, 77, 104, 113; 2
Mercurey 16
Merlot 14, 17, 35, 77; 17
Metala 63, 87; 86
Meursault 16, 35, 71, 104
Meursault-Charmes 75
Michigan 65
Minervois 17, 35
Minho 35, 85
mis en bouteilles 57, 117, 118, 119
Missouri 65
Missouri Riesling 19
mixing wines 69, 71–3
Moët et Chandon 28–9, 119; 119
Monbazillac 35, 98
Monterey Vineyards 16
Montilla 30, 89
Montrachet 13, 16, 104
Morey-St Denis 75
Morgon 105
Móri Ezerjó 81
Moscatel de Setúbal 85
Moscato 30
Mosel 18, 34, 35, 39, 58, 81, 87, 93, 114
Mosel-Saar-Ruwer 105
Moselle 25, 65, 71, 81
Moulin-à-Vent 105
Mousseux 120
Mouton Cadet 105
Müller-Thurgau 17, 71, 85, 118; 17
mulling wine 73; 73
Muscadelle de Bordelais 19
Muscadet 18, 34, 35, 71, 89, 93, 115, 120, 121
Muscat 18, 35, 71, 77, 98, 115; 18
Muscato 35
Muscatel 30
must 22, 120, 122
Myr 73; 72

Nahe 81, 105
Nantes 18, 71
Napa Valley 28, 34, 65, 85
Navarra 35, 83
Nebbiolo 35, 81
Neckar 58

négociant 52, 57, 120
New Jersey 65
New York 13, 65
Nicolet 69
Nierstein vineyard 58, 71, 81; 58
Niersteiner 35
Niersteiner Gutes Domtal 105
noble rot, 19, 116; 120
Nuits St Georges 77, 104

Oberrheim 58
Ockfener Bockstein Beerenauslese 13
oenology 120
Ohio 65
Oporto 8, 39, 63, 101
Orvieto 19, 35, 75, 81, 98; 74
over the top 120
oxidized wine 120

Palatinate, the 81, 97, 105
Palomino 18, 29; 18
Passe-tout-Grains, Bourgogne 94
Passito 35
pasteurization 120
Pauillac 104
Pécs Olasz Riesling 81
Penedes 35
pétillance 57, 71, 118, 120
Petit Sirah 19, 35
Phelps, Joseph 16
Piesporter 35
phylloxera 120
Piedmont 16, 81
Pineau de Charentes 30
Pinot Blanc 18, 85; 18
Pinot Meunier 14, 27
Pinot Noir 13, 14, 18, 26, 27, 34, 35, 71, 75, 77; 12, 18
Pomerol 16, 56, 77, 104
Pommard 104, 117; 117
Pope punch 73
port 8, 28, 29, 30, 63, 65, 69, 73, 89, 97, 98, 101, 113, 114, 116, 118; 28, 100
Pouilly-Fuissé 16, 35, 51, 71, 75, 81
Pouilly-Fumé 19, 35, 89, 93
Pouilly-Vinzelles 71
poultry and game and wine 75, 77–8, 79, 81–2, 83, 85, 87, 89, 90–1, 94–7; 74
pressing 22, 25, 27, 120; 25, 27, 120
primeur 120
Priorato 35
Provençe 19, 26, 77, 78, 81, 93, 94, 105, 115
Puglia 60
Puligny-Montrachet 104
punch 67, 73; 66

Punt e Mes 69

Qualitätswein bestimmter Anbangebiete 52, 58
Qualitätswein mit Pradikat 52, 58, 81
Quarts de Chaume 98
Quincy 19

racking 25, 120, 121
Reichensteiner 85
Rémy Martin 30
reserva 63, 120
reserve 120
restaurants, wine in 103–7
Retsina 94
Rheims 27, 47, 78–9, 121
Rheingau, the 52, 81, 93, 97, 105, 119, 121
Rheinhessen 22, 71, 81, 105
Rheinpfalz-Palatinate 105
Rheinpfalz Spätlese 94
Rhine 18, 58, 65, 71, 81, 85, 119, 121
Rhône Valley 14, 19, 25, 56, 77, 81, 89, 94, 105, 113, 122
Richebourg 104
Rieslaner 85
Riesling 16, 17, 18–19, 34, 35, 71, 73, 81, 85, 89, 93, 97, 120; 18, 70
rince cochon 71
Rioja 17, 35, 39, 62, 83, 94, 120; 38, 83
riserva 53, 60, 120
Rivaner 85
Roodeberg 35
Rosé d'Anjou 71
Roussillon 17, 30, 35, 77, 113
Ruländer 35

St Émilion 19, 35, 56, 77, 94, 104, 106, 117
St Estèphe 35
St Julien 35, 104
St Malo 15; 15
St Raphael 69
Saint Véran 7, 71, 75; 6
Sancerre 19, 35, 81, 93, 113, 115
Sangiovese 14, 19, 35
Sanlúcar de Barrameda 67
Sardinia 19
Saumur 16, 34, 35, 73, 115, 120, 121; 115
Sauternes 19, 25, 33, 35, 56, 65, 77–8, 93, 98, 104, 105, 116; 4–5; 99
Sauvignon Blanc 19, 35, 93; 19
Savennières 16, 93
Savigny-les-Beaunes 75
Savoie 81
Scharlachberg 58

Schiller 34
Schloss Vollrads 121; *121*
Schönburger 85
seafood and wine 18, 71, 75, 77–8, 81, 82, 83, 85, 87, 89, 90–1, 93–4; *83, 92, 93*
sec 57, 98, 120
sediment 121; *121*
Sekt 28, 71, 121
Selestat 69
Sémillon 19, 33, 35, 63, 77, 98; *19*
Sercial 30
serving wine 37–47, 87
Sétubal 18, 85
Seyval Blanc 85
sherry 8, 18, 29–30, 41, 45, 49, 65, 67–9, 73, 87, 97, 98, 101, 113, 114, 116, 118; *67, 86*
Shiraz 35, 75, 85, 87, 89, 94, 115; *86*
Sirah *see* Syrah
Soave 19, 35, 71, 81, 89
sommeliers 103, 106, 121
soup and wine 87, 89, 90–1, 93; *86, 93*
South Caroline 65
sparkling wines 26–9, 39–41, 43–5, 46–7, 49, 69–71, 73, 89, 98, 118, 121; *43, 70*
Spätlese wines 35, 52, 58, 93, 94, 97
spritzig 120
stains, removing wine 46
Steen 16, 35, 85
Steinwein 81
stoppers 45; *45*
storing wine 46–7, 106, 109, 117; *46–7, 106*
Süssreserve 81

Suze 69
Sylvaner 17, 19, 34, 35, 71, 81, 89, 93, 116; *19*
Syrah 16, 19; *19*
Szekszárd 81

Tahbilk 85
Tain l'Hermitage 19
tannin 13, 21, 25, 77, 121
tastes of wines 33–4; *35*
Tavel 17, 71, 77
temperature of wine, serving 39–41
thin wine 121
Tokay 16, 35, 41, 63, 65, 71, 81, 98, 113, 116; *41*
tonic wines 113–14
Torgiano 35, 82
Touraine 16, 79, 116, 120
Traminer 33, 81, 97
Trebbiano 14, 19, 35, 71
Trocken wines 35
Trockenbeerenauslese 35, 58
Tursan 81
Tuscany 8, 19, 81

Ugni Blanc 19
Umbria 81

Valdepeñas 35, 83, 97
Valdeorras 83
Valpolicella 35, 81, 97
varietal wine 121–2
vegetables and wine 78, 82, 83, 85; *78*
Veneto 71, 81
Verdicchio 35, 81, 89

vermouth 29, 30, 41, 68, 69, 73, 118; *31, 68*
Vernaccia 35
Verona 71, 81
Veuve Cliquot 27, 47, 121; *47*
Vienne 77
Vila Nova de Gaia 8, 28, 30
Vin Delimité de Qualité Supérieure 54, 77, 78, 121
vin de paille 122
vin de pays 54, 120
vin de table 22–5
vin ordinaire 14, 54, 122
vin rosé 71
vines *see* grapes
vinhos maduros 85
vinhos verdes 71, 85, 89; *70*
vinification 21–30, 122
vintages 105, 120, 122, 123
Virginia 65
viticulture 21–2, 26, 122; *26*
vitis vinifera 122
Volnay 34, 104
Vosne-Romanée 104
Vouvray 16, 35, 71, 79, 93, 113; *79*
VSO 121
VSOP 121

Washington 65
Winkel 121
Württemburg 81

yeast 122

Zell 58; *58*
Zinfandel 16, 19, 35, 85, 94